MORE THAN HIS GOD CARD

Brian accurately and skillfully helps us to understand and appreciate the meaning of Jesus' miracles. It's profoundly encouraging to apply these truths to our lives. After reading this book, you'll never look at the miracles of Jesus the same.

—David K. Hodge
Senior Vice President for North American Ministries,
Walk Thru the Bible

If joyful, original, logical, and clear enlargement of mind about the miracles of Jesus grabs your interests, this is your book.

—Gayle Erwin, author of *The Jesus Style*

Insightful and convicting, this book is a great resource and is most definitely worth the read! Its examination of Jesus' miracles takes you to a deeper understanding of His character as you are drawn into these incredible stories. Expect new insights and a new perspective you may not have seen before.

—Matt Williams
author and Teaching Pastor/Directional Leader,
Grace Church, Greenville, South Carolina

MORE THAN HIS GOD CARD

WHAT JESUS WANTS YOU TO KNOW ABOUT HIM AS REVEALED IN HIS MIRACLES

Brian Onken

AMBASSADOR INTERNATIONAL
GREENVILLE, SOUTH CAROLINA & BELFAST, NORTHERN IRELAND
www.ambassador-international.com

More Than His God Card

What Jesus Wants You to Know About Him as Revealed in His Miracles

ISBN: 978-1-62020-276-0
eISBN: 978-1-62020-378-1

Cover Design & Page Layout by Hannah Nichols
eBook Conversion by Anna Raats

AMBASSADOR INTERNATIONAL
Emerald House
427 Wade Hampton Blvd.
Greenville, SC 29609, USA
www.ambassador-international.com

AMBASSADOR BOOKS
The Mount
2 Woodstock Link
Belfast, BT6 8DD, Northern Ireland, UK
www.ambassadormedia.co.uk

The colophon is a trademark of Ambassador

For my Dad, who couldn't find the words to talk about his relationship with Jesus until shortly before his death.

CONTENTS

ACKNOWLEDGMENTS

THESE REFLECTIONS ON THE MIRACLES of Jesus have been a work in progress for many years. Exploring the Gospels with fellow friends of Jesus has been a part of my life for a long time. The numerous conversations and studies with brothers and sisters in Christ at Calvary Chapel of Redlands, Fullerton Evangelical Free Church, Evangelical Free Church of Orange, Calvary Church in Placentia, the Anaheim Vineyard, Church of the Woods in Lake Arrowhead, and Southside Fellowship in Greenville, have shaped and enriched my life and have been the laboratory in which these thoughts have been distilled. The list of individual names would be too long, but the gratitude for the journey we have been on together is heartfelt.

INTRODUCTION

WITH A FOCUS ON HIM

"You search the Scriptures because you think that in them you have eternal life; it is these that testify about Me; and you are unwilling to come to Me so that you may have life."

—John 5:39–40

JESUS IS AT THE HEART of the Christian life. You may say this is obvious, but how often, and how quickly, we can lose sight of this simple truth.

For example, learning to manage money biblically and discovering how to raise a Christian family are good things. But when the focus drifts from Jesus—who He is and what He does for us—to "ten steps to this" or "the secret of that," we move from living life *with* Jesus to doing life *for* Jesus (perhaps in the hope of gaining a few blessings along the way). This is a costly shift, which redirects the focus of our lives away from Him and back onto us.

But the Christian life really is all about Jesus. Growing to know Him better. Learning to love Him more. Seeking to follow

Him closer. Noticing what He's doing. Discovering what He's like, and even what He likes.

I am, and have long been, on a journey to get to know Jesus better. A significant part of my journey involves delving into the Scriptures. Jesus makes it clear, however, that our reading should be more than just searching for answers and key life principles. He even goes so far as to chastise the religious leaders of His day for taking that approach. They knew the Scriptures, they were diligent in their study, and yet, they were missing the point.

Jesus said, "You search the Scriptures because you think that in them you have eternal life . . . and you are unwilling to come to Me, that you may have life" (John 5:39-40). Although Jesus was making a direct reference to the Old Testament Scriptures, the same is true of the New: the whole Bible speaks of Jesus and He, therefore, is to be our focus of study.

I am continually fascinated by the Gospel accounts of the life and ministry of this One, the friend of our souls. One dimension of those Gospel accounts is the record of His miracles. Many saints, some better acquainted with Him and better students of His Word than I, have written about His miracles. But as I teach through the life of Jesus time and again, and as I grapple with what His miracles tell us about Him, I am finding that Jesus' compelling acts of power and grace may not be fully understood.

A COMMON MISCONCEPTION ABOUT HIS MIRACLES

> You know of Jesus of Nazareth, how God anointed Him with the Holy Spirit and with power, and how He went about doing good, and healing all who were oppressed by the devil; for God was with Him.
>
> —Acts 10:38

Most people are familiar with at least a few of Jesus' miracles. Take a brief pause from your reading and think through a short list of His miracles. What comes to mind?

Jesus healed and delivered many people from demonic spirits. He had power over the wind and the water. He changed water into wine and multiplied bread and fish. He even brought the dead back to life.

What can you recall about His miracles? Who does He touch? How does He do it? What are the details? And—perhaps most important to our study together—what do His miracles *mean*?

It wouldn't take long to find a commentary or a book on the works of Jesus that claims that His miracles prove His divinity. Often, the treatment of Jesus' miracles runs along the lines of, "And Jesus did a miracle showing He has authority over nature and, thus, proving He is God."[1] It is easy to think that Jesus' miracles were simply Him pulling out His "God card." But, if we stop and actually consider this line of reasoning, it becomes clear that something is amiss.

Glancing at a miracle can be like looking into the headlights of an oncoming car. We can feel dazed by the brightness. But if we're content to simply leave after being dazzled by the miracle itself, then we risk walking away short-sighted, missing the fuller message that Jesus desires to communicate.

AN INCONSISTENT APPROACH

What about miracles in the lives of others who walked with God? We don't hear commentators discussing the divinity of Peter or Paul. (See, for example, Acts 5:15 or 19:11–12.)[2] And no one is arguing that when Elijah called down fire from heaven he was showing "he has authority over nature . . . proving he is God." (See 2 Kings 1:10.)

In many cases, Jesus' miracles, in themselves, are not unique. Several other men raised individuals from the dead. (For example: Elisha in 2 Kings 4:32–36; Peter in Acts 9:40; Paul in Acts 20:9–10.) Other men healed the sick. (For example: Elisha in 2 Kings 5:13–14; the many accounts of healing in Acts.) And God's agents even controlled nature. (For example: Moses in Exodus 15:25; Elisha in 2 Kings 6:5–6; Paul in Acts 28:3–6.)[3]

Rather than getting into a lengthy discussion of the meaning of miracles in general (after all, there are other works that discuss miracles in such a light)[4], let's turn directly to the Gospels and discover the meaning of the miracles Jesus did. What is compelling is that the "God card" doesn't seem to be the motivation behind Jesus' miracles—at least not in the way it is often understood.

WHAT JESUS SAID ABOUT HIS WORKS

"Have I been so long with you, and yet you have not come to know Me, Philip? He who has seen Me

> has seen the Father; how can you say, 'Show us the Father?'"
>
> —John 14:9

In John chapter five, Jesus heals a man on the Sabbath. As a result, the religious leaders charge Him with the offense of doing "work"—something they saw as forbidden on the Sabbath. Jesus responded, "My Father is working until now, and I Myself am working" (John 5:17). To further explain what He meant by this, He continued, in verse 19:

> Truly, truly, I say to you, the Son can do nothing of Himself, unless it is something He sees the Father doing; for whatever the Father does, these things the Son also does in like manner.

What is He saying? Well, we could take this simply to mean, "Jesus is God", which of course is a biblically-true statement, but that's not what Jesus is intending here. Minimally, Jesus is identifying His "works" (that is, His miracles) with what He sees the Father doing. He does these miracles because they are the things the Father is doing. Thus the miracles are a revelation of the Father.[5]

This seems to be the point Jesus makes later when He is talking with some of His closest followers in the upper room. Jesus has already shared with His disciples that access to the Father can only come through Him. He has affirmed that He will be going to prepare a place for them with the Father. But Philip says to Him,

"Lord, show us the Father, and it is enough for us" (John 14:8). Jesus replies to Phillip:

> "Have I been so long with you, and yet you have not come to know Me, Philip? He who has seen Me has seen the Father; how can you say, 'Show us the Father?' Do you not believe that I am in the Father, and the Father is in Me? The words that I say to you I do not speak on My own initiative, but the Father abiding in Me does His works. Believe Me that I am in the Father and the Father is in Me; otherwise believe because of the works themselves."
>
> —John 14:9–11

Jesus' words address His nature and His miracles, but Jesus never said it the way we seem to want to take it: "The works I do, they prove that I am God."

At this point, you may be thinking, "Well, since Jesus is God and since the miracles do at least indicate something of His relationship with the Father, why is there any problem with concluding that His miracles are, in some sense, the 'God card'?" Good question. Here's my answer.

If we think of miracles only as proof when Jesus intends them to convey a message, we will miss out on some of what He truly desires for us to understand. We could find ourselves unintentionally overlooking a vital part of Jesus' communication to us.

The people we meet in the Gospel stories don't typically come to the conclusion that Jesus' miracles prove He is God. Reread the Gospels with an eye on the crowd's reactions to Jesus' miracles. Sometimes they aren't sure what to make of them (e.g., Mark 1:27), sometimes they're confused about what the miracles do reveal about Jesus (e.g., Mark 4:11), and sometimes they miss His point all together and give little attention to what Jesus is trying to reveal through His words and works (e.g., John 9:24–29).

Please don't miss this (because, apparently, many in Jesus' day did!). Jesus longs to speak to us—not only in *what He said* but also in *what He did*. And a large portion of what He did was to do the miraculous.

Jesus' miracles do provide evidence that He and the Father "are one," affirming He is God.[6] But if the only thing we conclude from watching Jesus heal, deliver, and control nature is, "Oh, He's God, He can do those things," then there is a strong chance we've missed some life-altering messages from Jesus.

It is not my intention to exhaustively treat the miracles of Jesus; that would take a larger book, a longer life, and a greater mind than mine. But I do hope that through the window of these miraculous wonders we will be able to catch a fresh glimpse of our gracious and wonderful Friend, who chose to come and bring us life. It is my prayer that through this miracle study we will discover a radical and invigorating portrait of Jesus, and that through His self-revealing acts we will experience a renewed and refreshing intimacy with our Savior and Friend.

So, let's dive in with Jesus' first miracle—a "sign" He did for a clear and stated purpose.

CHAPTER ONE

AND SO IT BEGINS . . .

THE WEDDING FEAST IN CANA

This beginning of His signs Jesus did in Cana of Galilee, and manifested His glory, and His disciples believed in Him.

—John 2:11

ALMOST EVERYONE ACKNOWLEDGES THAT JESUS did miracles and that amazing things happened around Him. But what if you could do one of the things that Jesus did? What would you choose? Heal people? Walk on water? Maybe raise the dead?

I have asked many people this question, and what surprises me is that I have never heard, "The wedding miracle; the one when Jesus turns water into wine."[7] In fact, I've discovered this miracle to be largely overlooked. It doesn't seem important. But to skip over this miracle is to miss something critical. This water-into-wine miracle was Jesus' first miracle and, as such, it sets the stage for all that follows.[8]

FIRST THINGS FIRST

First impressions do matter. People desire a respectable first impression so that a new relationship starts off on the right foot. The first page of a novel, the first day at a new job, the first date with that special someone are all significant. So it shouldn't surprise us that Jesus would use His first miracle to help us understand what He's all about.

> And on the third day there was a wedding in Cana of Galilee; and the mother of Jesus was there; and Jesus was also invited, and His disciples, to the wedding. And when the wine gave out, the mother of Jesus said to Him, "They have no wine." And Jesus said to her, "Woman, what do I have to do with you? My hour has not yet come." His mother said to the servants, "Whatever He says to you, do it."
>
> Now there were six stone water pots set there for the Jewish custom of purification, containing twenty or thirty gallons each. Jesus said to them, "Fill the water pots with water." And they filled them up to the brim. And He said to them, "Draw some out now, and take it to the headwaiter." And they took it to him. And when the headwaiter tasted the water which had become wine, and did not know where it came from (but the servants who had drawn the water knew), the headwaiter called the bridegroom, and said to him, "Every man serves the good wine first, and when men have drunk freely, then that which is poorer; you have kept the good wine until now."

> This beginning of His signs, Jesus did in Cana of Galilee, and manifested His glory, and His disciples believed in Him.
>
> —John 2:1–11

THERE'S MORE TO THE STORY

Some approach this passage as an allegory[9]—as if Jesus is conveying a message in picture form. The "good wine" represents the new Christianity that Jesus is bringing. The water pots represent either the ritual approach to faith found in the Judaism of Jesus' day or any man-made approach to being cleansed from sin. Thus interpreted, this miracle is foretelling Jesus' message of Good News. Read this way, the story supposedly informs us that Jesus' teaching should be embraced in the same way the headwaiter welcomed the fine wine.

This may not be an altogether inappropriate way to understand this miracle. Jesus *is* doing something new. In Matthew 9:16–17 Jesus even offers a couple of short parables—including one about new wine and old wine skins—that supports this kind of idea.

But what about those at the wedding feast? Would they have concluded that Jesus' teaching was going to overshadow the religious practices and teachings of the day? Probably not. So how would they (and those to whom John is writing) have interpreted Jesus' turning water into wine?[10]

Jesus did not do this miracle capriciously. He did it for a reason. But what message did His witnesses walk away with?

John helps us make sense of this miracle when he explains: "This beginning of His signs, Jesus did in Cana of Galilee, and manifested His glory, and His disciples believed in Him" (John 2:11).

First, we see that this miracle is a "sign." That's not the same as an allegory. John isn't saying that Jesus is sending a coded picture message about what's to come. But the phrase "beginning of His signs" does suggest that this act is not an end in itself.

According to John, Jesus did this miracle to "manifest His glory." In reading these words we must be careful not to attach our own preconceived ideas to what John is saying. There's a tendency—as was explained in the introduction—to look at this miracle of Jesus and say, "Wow, look at His creative power over nature. He must be God!" But John doesn't tell us that Jesus did this to "prove that He was God."

If Jesus had intended this sign to be a powerful declaration of His divinity, why do it for such a small audience? How many knew what happened with the water? The servants who filled the water pots and the handful of disciples who joined Jesus at the banquet. If Jesus was intending this "first of His signs" to be proof that He was God in the flesh, why do it in a corner, without a clear audience, in such an obscure way?

Put yourself at the wedding feast. If you *did* find out that Jesus was responsible for the impressive wine, and that He provided it in a different (even miraculous) way, would you have jumped to the conclusion: "Jesus changed water into wine. Well then, He must be God."? Yeah, me neither. And I doubt those who were there made that mental leap.

So what does John mean when he writes that Jesus did this to reveal His glory? When we talk of someone's "glory" we are referring to the qualities or characteristics of their greatness.[11] To manifest the glory of someone is to put his or her greatness on display. Thus, this miracle is putting some facet of Jesus' greatness on display.[12] Not only does Jesus reveal a piece of his character in this miracle but He also provokes a response: "His disciples believed in Him."

John doesn't always use *believing* to mean "saving faith."[13] A thorough reading of John's Gospel helps us see that *believing* means here "to trust in, to depend on, and to put confidence in Jesus"—a growing, ever-increasing trust in Jesus Himself.[14] In his Gospel, John invites us into a deeper understanding of what believing is all about. So, when we read *believing* in John's Gospel, we need to think about someone "coming to trust Jesus more."

IMAGINE

So, we are told Jesus did this "first sign" to put an aspect of His character on display. And His followers came to trust Him more. But what *did* Jesus reveal about His character?

Jesus is a guest at this wedding. He is not responsible for or expected to meet any celebration needs. But, He does. And He does it in an incredible way.

In Jesus' day, wedding feasts lasted for several days, and the best wine was always served first (in order to make a good first impression). When the guests were comfortable, and their pallets were tempered by the best the host had to offer, the headwaiter could bring out the lesser quality items without fear of insult or displeasure.

This is a rough calculation, but Jesus created around 180 gallons of exceptionally fine wine. So, Jesus produces 180 gallons of wine largely in secret. It's not even clear if anyone other than the few servants and disciples ever learned what happened. So obviously Jesus isn't looking to make a stir with this miracle. But He is communicating with His disciples.

How would you describe this unexpected wedding present? What does it demonstrate or show us about Jesus? I've tried to find a simple way to capture what is seen in this moment. I think it could be summed up by saying that this was an example of *extravagant grace*.

OVER THE TOP

Jesus met a need that wasn't His concern. And He met it with 180 gallons of wine. He didn't just provide a little bit of wine, just enough to get by—He provided 180 gallons of the best wine! That's quite a generous wedding gift.

Have you ever received an unexpected gift from someone who went overboard in his or her expenditure or effort? You probably felt stunned and words failed you as you tried to fathom your friend's generosity. This is what Jesus did. Jesus' gift is incredibly generous. Jesus is extravagantly gracious! And He does this miracle to put His graciousness on display.

Jesus is an over-the-top gift giver. Do you believe that? Do you see that Jesus wants you to trust Him and to believe that He is extravagantly generous? I wouldn't dare put this idea forward if I was not convinced that it is something Jesus desires us to know. Jesus performed this miracle to convince us—everyone who wants to be His disciple—that He gives . . . lavishly, freely, wonderfully.

Jesus' whole life was one radical gift of love . . . for you. He came to serve you (Mark 10:45). He came to give you life abundantly (John 10:10). He came to buy you out, freely, from your bondage to sin (Matthew 20:28; John 8:34–36). And this miracle is only the first chapter of the most marvelous story ever told—the account of Jesus' love for us. For you.

Yet how easy it is for me to slip into thinking that God is like Scrooge. That He's tightfisted with His blessings, holding back until I have my life fully under control. Sadly, many Christians share my struggle and thus approach God hesitantly. Believing God to be stingy, our minds and hearts question whether He genuinely intends good for us.

But this miracle proves that He does. And we must take this powerful truth of extravagant grace to heart because honestly, this "generous gift giver" theme never leaves the life of Jesus.

Jack Hayford, pastor of Church on the Way, in his book *Moments with Majesty*, writes:

> From the moment of my entry into the saving life Jesus has given me through the cross, all the way through my lifetime of learning to walk in His love and power . . . it's all grace. He gives it. . . . As the hymn writer put it, "He giveth, and giveth, and giveth again." . . . The resource from which He gives [is] boundless, measureless, unlimited, abundant, almighty, and eternal. Be comforted and

> emboldened in your faith, friend. God has gifts for you and in quantities you never dreamed.[15]

Think with me about finding yourself in a time of need. Facing the need, you remember two friends. One is tight-fisted: he holds on to what he has with little apparent gladness in extending resources or grace to others. You other friend is open-handed: you've seen him generously and happily seek to meet needs in the lives of those he knows. Both have a proven character—a quality of life that is evident. When you think of these friends with regard to your need, who would you be more inclined to trust with your situation? Naturally, it would be the generous, gracious, and kind friend.

In the same way, is it not easier, simpler, and wiser to trust the One who has shown Himself to be gracious and kind and generous?

THE FIRST SNAPSHOT

There it is, the first snapshot in our photo album: Jesus' first miracle.

Jesus has revealed His extravagant grace. He's stirred His followers to begin to trust in Him. And He's set the tone for what's to come.

When I consider Jesus' extravagant grace, the same feelings that undoubtedly stirred in the hearts of those early friends of Jesus stir in me. I am impressed with Jesus' generosity and kindness. And like them, I find myself wanting to get to know Jesus better and, perhaps, even trust Him with my needs, my situations, and my life.[16]

What does this miracle, this beautiful portrayal of Jesus' abundant provision and love, stir inside of you?

REFLECTING ON THIS TRUTH

FOR PERSONAL REFLECTION:

1. If this is your first time seeing Jesus as a generous gift giver in this miracle—if before you merely saw this miracle as Jesus pulling out His "God card"—thank Him for showing you more of what He is like. And talk to Him about what you're discovering.

2. Since Jesus did this miracle to show more of Himself, ask Him to help you grasp what He is like. Be willing to swap out any ideas that don't do Him justice and ask Him to reveal an accurate picture of Himself.

3. In the letter to the Hebrews, we read about the essence of faith: "The one who comes to God must believe that He is, and that He is a rewarder of those who seek Him" (Hebrews 11:6). Do you believe that when you come to God you come to one who gives? One who gives lavishly? Spend some time in worship, reflecting and celebrating God for His generosity.

FOR GROUP DISCUSSION:

1. What are some benefits to seeing Jesus' miracles as a way He reveals His character? How could this perspective change the way you read His other miracles and the Gospels?

2. Do you think of Jesus as extravagantly gracious? Why or why not? How would your relationship with Him change if you

began to see Him as a Friend who desires to give you abundantly generous gifts?

3. What issues or struggles would be easier to surrender to Jesus' care if you saw Him as He is in this miracle story? Why?

CHAPTER TWO

WHAT DOES HE KNOW?

THE GREAT CATCH OF FISH

And Simon answered and said, "Master, we worked hard all night and caught nothing, but I will do as You say and let down the nets."

—Luke 5:5

IT'S EASY FOR US TO take the miracles in the Bible for granted. In fact there's a tendency to skim right over them and miss what's being said.

Most people are familiar with Israel's famous deliverance from slavery and from Egypt. It's found in the opening chapters of the book of Exodus, and it is a section full of excitement and drama as God shows up in miraculous ways.

God, through His chosen intermediary Moses, sends a series of ten plagues on Egypt. The plagues are powerful displays of God's power. But they are more than that. These ten plagues were specific and had particular targets in mind.

When Moses first asked Pharaoh to let God's people go, he refused, saying, "Who is Yahweh that I should obey His voice and let Israel go? I do not know Yahweh, and besides I will not let Israel go" (Exodus 5:2).[17] Pharaoh knew many gods; the Egyptians worshipped many gods. But Pharaoh said he didn't know the God of the Hebrews—the one called Yahweh.

God told Moses that He would prove Himself to be greater than the gods of Egypt. God was "executing judgment against all the gods of Egypt" (Exodus 12:12). The turning of water to blood is one example that illustrates His intentions. Moses, under God's direction, made all the water in Egypt unfit for consumption by turning it into blood (Exodus 7: 14–25). The Egyptian conjurors also duplicated something similar to what God accomplished through Moses, but His point was not lost.

So what is going on here? One commentator has this to say:

> Both the time and the place are of significance here. Pharaoh went out in the morning to the Nile, not merely to take a refreshing walk, or to bathe in the river, or to see how high the water had risen, but without doubt to present his daily worship to the Nile, which was honored by the Egyptians as their supreme deity. At this very moment the will of God with regard to Israel was declared to him; and for his refusal to comply with the will of the Lord as thus revealed to him, the smiting of the Nile with the staff made known to him the fact, that the God of the Hebrews was the true God, and possessed the power to turn the fertilizing water of this object of their highest worship into blood.[18]

God was strategically showing Himself in contrast to the gods of the Egyptians. In this plague on the Nile, He was demonstrating that He was greater than their river god, Hapi. Each of His ten plagues had a target.

That God acts with purpose is something we must remember when we look at Jesus' miracles. We need to look closely at what happens and the details given about Jesus' miracles because through those acts Jesus reveals something about Himself. And attention to such details will help us make sense of the miracle to which we now turn.

THE EARLY DAYS OF FRIENDSHIP

Peter was one of Jesus' closest friends. But, like any good relationship, it would have taken time to develop. Sometimes, in reading the Gospels, we forget that we're reading a time-compressed account.

According to Scripture, Peter met Jesus along the shore of the Sea of Galilee before he was called to follow Him (as recorded in Matthew 4:18–20 and Mark 1:16–18). The book of John records one of Peter's earliest moments with Jesus.

> Again the next day John [the Baptist] was standing, and two of his disciples; and he looked upon Jesus as He walked, and said, "Behold, the Lamb of God!"
>
> And the two disciples heard him speak, and they followed Jesus. And Jesus turned and beheld them following, and said to them, "What do you seek?" And they said to Him, "Rabbi (which translated means Teacher), where are You staying?"

> He said to them, "Come and you will see." They came therefore and saw where He was staying, and they stayed with Him that day, for it was about the tenth hour.
>
> One of the two who heard John speak, and followed Him, was Andrew, Simon Peter's brother. He found first his own brother Simon, and said to him, "We have found the Messiah (which translated means Christ)." He brought him to Jesus. Jesus looked at him, and said, "You are Simon the son of John; you shall be called Cephas (which translated means Peter)."
>
> —John 1:35–42

This is a simple start to Jesus' relationship with Peter. There is nothing necessarily miraculous about this encounter or about Peter's relationship with Jesus at this point in time. But things did change.

DOING WHAT COMES NATURALLY

That story in John is obviously not Peter's only encounter with Jesus. During Jesus' early stage of ministry we see Peter again. This time, we do see a remarkable miracle. Initially, Jesus' actions might seem like a capricious display of power. But, knowing Jesus, this is unlikely.

> Now it came about that while the multitude were pressing around Him and listening to the word of God, He was standing by the lake of Gennesaret; and He saw two boats lying at the edge of the lake; but the fishermen had gotten

out of them, and were washing their nets. And He got into one of the boats, which was Simon's, and asked him to put out a little way from the land. And He sat down and began teaching the multitudes from the boat.

And when He had finished speaking, He said to Simon, "Put out into the deep water and let down your nets for a catch."

And Simon answered and said, "Master, we worked hard all night and caught nothing, but at Your bidding I will let down the nets."

And when they had done this, they enclosed a great quantity of fish; and their nets began to break; and they signaled to their partners in the other boat, for them to come and help them. And they came, and filled both of the boats, so that they began to sink.

But when Simon Peter saw that, he fell down at Jesus' feet, saying, "Depart from me, for I am a sinful man, O Lord!" For amazement had seized him and all his companions because of the catch of fish which they had taken; and also James and John, sons of Zebedee, who were partners with Simon. And Jesus said to Simon, "Do not fear, from now on you will be catching men."

And when they had brought their boats to land, they left everything and followed Him.

—Luke 5:1–11

To understand what is happening, what Jesus is doing, and why it had such an impact on Peter, we need to know a little about fishing.

If you were to visit the villages along the Sea of Galilee in Peter's day, you would have found many fishermen. It was a common trade and each man followed two basic fishing strategies. The first involved standing in shallow water and casting a net by hand into the water where the fish were seen. (Peter used this approach in Mark 1:16.) Then the fishermen would draw in the net, ensnaring the fish.

In the passage above, Peter had been using the second approach, called a "drag net." This method required a boat and deeper waters. Drag nets were made of sturdy rope, and because these nets were thick, and because fish are not entirely stupid, they could not simply toss them into the sea with the hope of catching something.

These nets required fishermen to work at night, when the fish could not see them. The boats would sit in somewhat shallow waters so the fish could not swim under, or around, the nets. After the fishermen lowered their nets into the water, they hung a light on the opposite side of the boat, to draw the fish in close. It was a simple technique, but it was smart and usually successful.

Now back to the miracle. Because of the crowd on the shore, Jesus asked Peter for the use of his boat. If Peter were to put off from the shore a little way, it would provide Jesus with a natural amphitheater, as the water would carry His words to those seated along the curve of the lake. Peter, willing to be of assistance, takes Jesus out in his boat for the duration of the teaching. After His teaching, Jesus makes an astounding request. (It may not sound that extreme to us, but it would have to Peter.)

Jesus says, "Put out into the deep water and let down your nets for a catch."

There is no doubt that Peter was surprised at this request. It was one thing for Jesus to ask for the use of the boat and for Peter to pull out away from the shore. Peter could make sense of that request. But this? Jesus, a carpenter and teacher, was telling him, an accomplished fisherman, how to catch fish. And Jesus' suggested method was ridiculous!

No one fished in deep waters; the fish would go under or around the nets. No one fished in the middle of the day; the nets would be visible and only blind fish would swim into them!

You can even sense Peter's reluctance in his words:

"Master,[19] *we* worked hard all *night* and caught nothing . . ." Which, put bluntly, means, "We, who are fisherman, tried, at the most opportune time, and didn't catch a thing."

Peter continues, "But at *Your* bidding I will let down the nets." What he's really saying is, "Let it be clear that we aren't doing this because we think it's a good idea. Everyone needs to know we are doing this foolish thing only because You asked." Peter acquiesces; with some reluctance he gives in to the request.

I can almost see Peter's eyes roll as he heads out toward the deeper part of the lake. And I can envision the other fishermen looking out at Peter as he tries to avoid their incredulous stares.

Together, Jesus and Peter finally reach the spot. Jesus asks him to lower the nets. And then, the unimaginable happens.

It didn't happen instantaneously; the fish didn't jump into the boat. Peter, with his hands on the nets and his eyes on his provocative passenger, began to feel the weight of the net increase.

Something was happening. The net was either snagged on something or . . .

Peter begins to pull. He can see the fish; dozens and dozens of them. Splashing and flailing in the net! He strains to keep from losing his grip. He's pulling fish out of the net and into the boat as quickly as he can. And Jesus is at his side, smiling and helping.

It's unimaginable. What must be going through Peter's mind as, soaked in sweat and heart racing, he finds himself up to his knees in fish?

Peter hauls in a catch of fish so immense that his boat cannot handle the weight. Another boat is signaled[20] to come and help, and both almost sink because of the weight of the haul.

ONE FISH, TWO FISH, RED FISH, BLUE FISH

So, what's the meaning of all of this? Is Jesus flippantly zapping fish into Peter's net for fun? Probably not. Perhaps Peter is to conclude from this display that Jesus is God. But that doesn't align with the Gospel account either.

It's clear, when Peter's life is examined, that this wasn't the miracle that convinced him of Jesus' divinity. We have to walk with Peter and Jesus through a substantial portion of the Gospels before Peter confesses Jesus as the Christ or comes to recognize Him as divine. So what *is* going on here? What does this miracle show us about Jesus?

There are two lines of thought worth pursuing when it comes this miracle. Let's take them separately.

The first is rooted in the understanding that wherever Jesus went, He responded to needs. He didn't use His power to only impress or wow people. When He acted, He did it out of compassion and to meet needs.[21] With that in mind, we can rightly ask: Is there a need that this catch of fish will meet?

In a short time, Jesus intends to ask Peter to sign up as a "fisher of men." What will that mean? It will mean that Peter will have to radically alter his business practices. He won't be able to give himself to fishing each day in order to make a living, as had been his habit.

We know from the Scriptures that Peter was married. We don't know much about his family life, but he clearly had some family. If Jesus is going to take Peter away from his daily work to do other things, there will be a great need left to meet. Jesus knew this and He did something about it.

Jesus provided for Peter in such an abundant way that when He asked Peter to follow Him, Peter could, fully knowing that the needs of his family were met. This catch was more than a few days' supply. Such a sizable load of fish would have met his family's demands for some time.

Jesus did not simply "bless" Peter with an abundance of fish. Jesus provided Peter with this catch so that Peter could follow Him more freely.

Sometimes I wonder if Jesus really understands what He's asking of me when He calls me to follow Him. I wonder if He knows that I have obligations and responsibilities. After all, I can't just ignore my responsibilities and family needs.

Some days my load feels overwhelming: the obligations, the responsibilities, the tasks, the demands. People are counting on me, leaning on me, expecting things of me. And then Jesus speaks up, and He has different plans for my day. This is when I wonder, "Does He really *understand* my life?"

But in this miracle we see an answer to my question, to our question. This miracle shows me that Jesus did understand what Peter was facing. Jesus didn't call him to irresponsible living. Jesus provided what was needed so that, in a sensible way, Peter could follow.

This is wonderful to see in Jesus. But I believe there's something else going on in this miracle. And it's seen in Peter's reaction.

BEYOND AMAZEMENT

If you had been in the boat with these fishermen, how would you have responded? If you were a professional fisherman and someone helped you catch an unimaginable amount of fish, what would you have done?

Would you have cheered and whooped and hollered? Would you have jumped up and down, or stood speechless in astonishment, awed by the windfall of fish? Would you have posed for pictures with the record catch, hoping to make the front pages of the Capernaum Chronicle?

Peter responds with, "I don't want You around."

Luke tells us that Peter was "astonished." Although the English word *astonished* appears often in the Gospels, it varies from our understanding of the word. It's much greater than, "Wow, that was great! Can you do it again?" We see this by Jesus' response to Peter, "Do not fear." Why would Jesus say that? Why would Peter be afraid?

Let me suggest an approach to this miracle that seems to clarify what happened and why Peter responded in fear.

When Peter put out from the shore with Jesus, he was accommodating his new friend because he had the time to do so. Peter's work was done for the day; a little tidying up was all that remained.

But then, out at sea, Jesus makes His request. And now Peter, out in the middle of the day, is a bit uncomfortable. Peter responds, "We've fished all night . . ." Why tell this to Jesus? To remind Jesus that he, the fisherman, had already done all that could be done to bring in a catch.

Peter knows fishing. Jesus may know about religious things. Jesus may have great theological or philosophical insights. But He obviously doesn't know much about fishing. Professional fishermen don't fish in deep waters in the middle of the day!

I think Peter is fine with Jesus doing what Jesus knows best, as long as Jesus doesn't mess with what Peter knows best. Something like that must have been going through Peter's mind and heart as he pulled on the oars and headed out into the deeper waters.

Then it happens. Against everything Peter had known. A catch of a lifetime. And Peter's reply is humble and telling: "Depart from me, for I am a sinful man."

Why does he say that? Peter couldn't have understood that Jesus was God come in the flesh. As we have noticed already, you have to travel a good deal further into the Gospels before Peter arrives at this truth. So why does Peter want Jesus to leave?

Jesus knows Peter. Jesus knows his needs. Jesus knows Peter's business better than Peter does. I think this realization must have struck Peter. And then fear quickly followed.

What if Jesus, who apparently knows more than Peter imagined, also knew what kind of man Peter was? This is a frightening thought, that someone may know me, may know you, better than I know myself. Peter knew he wasn't worthy to be in the presence of such an amazing man. And he swiftly volunteers this admission and requests, "Depart from me . . . I am a sinful man."

KEEP YOUR DISTANCE

What a fascinating—and very true-to-life—picture we have here. Many of us wear masks as we go through life, hoping no one will see who we are or peer into the thoughts we think. We're aware of the brokenness inside of us, but we desperately hide it from others, convinced that if they knew they would start sprinting in the other direction. Like Peter, we are tempted to push people away when they get too close. "Stay away, keep your distance; I know me, and I am not sure I want you to know me better."

But Jesus ignores Peter's request. Jesus knows all of Peter's heart and He has decided that He wants an intimate and eternal friendship with this boisterous fisherman. So Jesus invites Peter to join Him, to become a "fisher of men."

This account is a remarkable miracle. Not simply because of the great catch of fish. That, of course, is amazing, and would have been cool to see. But what is even more wonderful is how Jesus demonstrates, through this miracle, His expansive understanding of Peter, the fisherman and sinner. Jesus knew exactly whom He was getting with Peter. Peter didn't need to wear a mask. He could be himself.

Let that sink in deep. Knowing Peter did not make Jesus want to run. No, He had the opposite reaction; He invited Peter to be with Him.

I SEE YOU

Later in the Gospels, Peter, in a moment of panic and fear, denies knowing Jesus. As Jesus faces crucifixion, Peter bails on Him. It is a sorrowful moment for the bold fisherman. And soon after Peter goes back to fishing, until Jesus shows up once again.

Read what happened next; this is found at the end of John's Gospel. After the resurrection, Jesus showed up on the shore and made breakfast for some of His disciples.

> So when they had finished breakfast, Jesus said to Simon Peter, "Simon, son of John, do you love Me more than these?"
>
> He said to Him, "Yes, Lord; You know that I love You."
>
> He said to him, "Tend my lambs." He said to him again a second time, "Simon, son of John, do you love Me?"
>
> He said to Him, "Yes, Lord; You know that I love You.
>
> He said to him the third time, "Simon, son of John, do you love Me?"
>
> Peter was grieved because He said to him the third time, "Do you love Me?" And he said to Him, "Lord, You know all things; You know that I love You."
>
> Jesus said to him, "Tend my sheep."
>
> —John 21:15–17 [22]

Do you notice what Peter consistently affirms throughout this exchange? Many Bible teachers call attention to Peter's reaffirmation of his love for Jesus. But did you also notice that, each time, Peter asserts that Jesus knows him, really knows him!

The journey to that realization may have started in the boat, some three years earlier, when Jesus acted in a tender but powerful display, and made it clear that He knew more about Peter's life than Peter ever imagined.

This miracle wasn't about fish. It was about Jesus showing Peter, "I know My business and I know yours, too."

Everyone, at some time, experiences the fear of being known. We know a lot about ourselves, and often we're not so sure we want someone else to know us quite that well.

But if we can get past the fear, a new world opens before us. There is a trust, a joy, and a freedom that comes when we begin living out who we really are, without pretense, in the presence of others. To be known well by another can be a freeing thing, particularly if the One who knows us so well has shown Himself to be a gracious, compassionate, wise, and competent Friend. Especially if, after knowing all about me, He still wants my companionship.

Is it possible that having Jesus really know me, and Peter and you, through and through, is a good thing? Or dare I suggest a great thing?

REFLECTING ON THIS TRUTH

FOR PERSONAL REFLECTION:

1. The fact that Jesus *knows* you can be a scary thought; it was for Peter. And Jesus really does know about your life, your needs, your business. In fact, He knows it all even better than you do. Pause a minute. Allow your shame and anxiety to pass, and rest in the comfort that He knows you, that He loves you, and that He is not going to take you somewhere without meeting your needs in a full and gracious way.

2. Has Jesus been calling you to a new adventure with Him? Have you heard His voice asking you to step out in some fresh way? Are you holding back because you're uncertain about real life concerns? I'm not suggesting that you be rash. But don't hold back from responding to His call out of worry that Jesus won't meet your daily needs. Think of those boats, nearly breaking under the load of fish. That's Jesus. He takes care of His own.

3. Jesus not only reveals His character in this miracle; He tells us how He wants to relate to us—without pretense. Read His words in Matthew 6:25–33, and talk to Him about being real, about resting in His provision, and about being comfortable with Him being your provider.

FOR GROUP DISCUSSION:

1. Does watching Jesus meet a need in Peter's life, even before Peter is aware of it, nudge you to trust Jesus more with your life? Why? How?

2. Would you have asked Jesus to leave (like Peter did) once you realized how much He might know about you? Why or why not?

3. Jesus really did know Peter, his strengths and weakness, his fears and needs. Still, Jesus wanted Peter to join up with Him. How does this impact or help you in your own journey with Jesus?

> to the priest and offer for your cleansing what Moses commanded, as a testimony to them." But he went out and began to proclaim it freely and to spread the news around, to such an extent that Jesus could no longer publicly enter a city, but stayed out in unpopulated areas; and they were coming to Him from everywhere.
>
> —Mark 1:40–45

At this point in the Gospel story, we know that Jesus could heal "various diseases" and that He cared for many who were ill. But we haven't yet heard of Jesus dealing with leprosy. To make sense of this account, it would be of benefit to know a little about that disease and how it was perceived in Jesus' day.[29]

The Old Testament provides us with a framework for understanding leprosy.[30] This disease infected the skin and tissues. As it developed, it would often leave the sick person scarred, even deformed. It was not only considered contagious, but it rendered the person ritually and spiritually "unclean."

This contagiousness and uncleanliness meant that those so afflicted could not live within normal community life. They settled into colonies of those similarly infected. Lepers could not participate in the regular worship of the people of Israel. They could not attend synagogue or go to the Temple. If a leper did attempt to come into a populated area, he would have to approach in a particular manner, crying out as he came, "Unclean!"

That background on leprosy can help us to not overlook a few other important items that go into making up this account.

Did you notice how the leper came to Jesus? Mark tells us that he "beseeched" Jesus. Each time Mark uses that word in his Gospel it carries the sense of a passionate plea—the idea of begging Jesus for something.[31] This leper also came "falling on his knees" before Jesus. In Mark we meet only one other person coming to Jesus on his knees.[32] It is clear from this language that the man is desperate. But is it only the severity of his affliction that drives this desperation? Or could there be something more?

Listen again to the leper's plea: "If You are willing, You can make me clean." What does this tell us about the leper's grasp of Jesus' ministry?

Undoubtedly, the leper has heard about Jesus' ministry of healing; the word had gone out into all the region of Galilee (Mark 1:28, 39). Although Jesus had brought healing to people with various diseases, there is no mention of Him having dealt with leprosy up to this point in time.

It could be that the leper is taking a risk. He is aware that Jesus can heal. But he may not be sure that Jesus can do anything about leprosy. He could well be wondering if Jesus is willing to get involved in this troublesome, spiritually complex problem. "*If* You are willing . . ." That is what the leper wonders—whether Jesus is going to be willing to address his particular need.

If you pause and look back over the recap we made of Mark's introduction to Jesus' ministry, you might notice a pattern.

Jesus entered the synagogue in Capernaum and taught in a powerful way and, subsequently, brought deliverance to a single demonized man. Leaving the synagogue, He entered Simon's mother-in-law's house where His companions told Jesus she was sick with a fever.

It's worth noting that they didn't ask Jesus to heal her. That should not be surprising, because at that point all Jesus' companions knew of Him was that He was a good teacher and had authority over a demon that was afflicting a man. They had no basis for assuming Jesus could do anything about physical illnesses. They took a risk—probably not sure what He would do—in telling Him about Peter's mom. And Jesus healed her.

It's worth noting that when word got out about what Jesus had done to help Simon's mother-in-law that the people of the town began bringing those who were sick with a whole variety of afflictions. But up until that point in time, Jesus had healed only one elderly woman infirm with a fever. It's not likely that those gathered around the door that evening were only sick old ladies with fevers. Those brought and those who were bringing the sick were taking risks—probably not sure what Jesus would or could do for others who were ill. And Jesus healed many and freed many from oppression.

Then we meet the leper. And it appears he was taking a risk as well. He knew Jesus had healed some. But he wasn't sure Jesus would get involved in his situation. Nevertheless, he approached Jesus. And the risk was worth it. Jesus cleansed and healed him.

WHAT LITTLE THEY KNEW

One thing that is so intriguing about these early moments of Jesus' public ministry is this dynamic of seeing something in

Jesus sufficient to drive someone to take a risk with Him—and to find that He responded so well to the step taken.

Simon and Andrew knew very little about Jesus, yet they ventured to tell Him about Simon's mother-in-law. The crowd had only a day's worth of information about Jesus and had seen Him do only a little, yet they ventured to bring to Him all manner of sick and afflicted. The leper knew a bit more but apparently was unclear about whether Jesus would do something about leprosy, yet he fell to the ground before Jesus, pleading for help.

In every one of these situations, the people knew so little. But the little they did know was enough to move them toward Jesus with their needs. And this nudges me to reflect upon my own life, my own struggles.

We know so much more about Jesus than did those who approached Him in Capernaum that weekend He began to minister. We have four Gospels full of accounts. We have numerous epistles that tell us about who Jesus is and all that He brings into our lives by grace. We have years of history where Jesus' ongoing ministry is evident in the life of His church.

We know so much. But is the much that we know enough to move us toward Jesus with our needs? Why are there things that I don't bring to Him? Why do I not take risks with Him? What did they see in Him that I don't see that enabled them to risk—in big ways and small ways—exposing their needs so that He might address those needs?

SOME ESSENTIAL PIECES

There are some details in this account that might help us see what those around Jesus recognized that would have encouraged them in their risk taking—and that can encourage us as well. When reading this account, our attention is naturally drawn to the healing itself—and it is remarkable, wonderful, amazing. But Mark tells us a bit more than merely reporting that Jesus healed a leper. Mark has his eyes on a few different Lego blocks necessary for building the story he is telling.

We need to look carefully at how Jesus healed this leper and what Jesus did after healing him, because those details are not only part of this miracle story, but they provide insight into Jesus that we need to see.[33]

Mark tells us: "Moved with compassion, Jesus stretched out His hand and touched him, and said to him, 'I am willing; be cleansed.'" Seemingly insignificant details, but startlingly important details if we take only a moment to notice.

Jesus is "moved with compassion." It's an interesting expression; the idea is that Jesus was "stirred in the gut." He felt something, seeing this man desperate and kneeling before Him. This little phrase helps us understand that Jesus does not go through His healing ministry in a mechanical or disinterested way. The leper before Him matters to Jesus.

Jesus "stretched out His hand." Apparently the leper was close, but Jesus still had to extend Himself to reach the man.[34] There is something personal, attentive, and active pictured in Mark's description of this moment. Jesus is not staying at arms' distance from this man's desperate need.

Jesus "touched him." This provocative action can be easily overlooked by modern readers. Lepers were unclean. Lepers lived apart from others. Lepers were devoid of human contact. And in healing this man, Jesus physically put His hand on the man.[35] Jesus is willing to be that "up close and personal" with not only a total stranger—but someone whom most other people would have avoided at all cost.

Jesus said to him, "I am willing." How wonderful those words must have sounded to that leper! Having taken a huge risk—working his way into the city and through the crowds—and then to hear those words! "Jesus *wants* to heal me!" There is nothing perfunctory or merely functional about what Jesus is doing.

Moving through Mark's Gospel and coming to this account, we will have already heard that Jesus can and does heal people. But Mark lingers here. Mark brings us close. He narrates details. He doesn't merely tell us that Jesus healed the man. He tells us so much more. And it is that "more" that might help us understand why people were so willing to risk with Jesus.

This snapshot of Jesus interacting with the leper is not an exception—it is a clear picture of who Jesus is and what He is like. When Simon informed Jesus about his mother-in-law's condition, it was *this Jesus* who went in to see her. When Jesus moved through the crowds outside of Simon's mother-in-law's house, it was *this Jesus* who those people met. And Mark wants us to see what all these who were taking risks with Jesus were seeing—they saw *this Jesus*.

Those Jesus ministers to matter to Him; He is moved by them and interested in them. Jesus reaches out and touches those who come to Him with needs; He is personal and attentive. Jesus does what He does because He wants to; He is not merely "doing a job."

How we need to see *this Jesus*! Personal, attentive, compassionate, up-close, engaged—not just a "healer," but *this* kind of man. That Jesus is truly this kind of man is pictured in the postscript to the healing. Do not overlook what happens after the healing, because Mark is calling our attention to something significant.

MORE THAN BUSY WORK

In reading the account of this healing, it's easy to either skip over or be puzzled by Jesus' words to the leper *after* He healed and cleansed the man. The miracle has already happened—the man was healed. What does it matter what Jesus tells the man after his healing? But if we think that, we will miss something crucial.

After the man is healed, Jesus "sternly warned him and immediately sent him away, and He said to him, 'See that you say nothing to anyone; but go, show yourself to the priest and offer for your cleansing what Moses commanded, as a testimony[36] to them.'"

Why does Jesus want the former leper to do this? Some people think that Jesus wants the man to witness to the priests—to tell them what Jesus has done for him and, in that way, promote Jesus' own ministry. But there are a few indicators that this might not be the case.

Jesus tells the man to "say nothing to anyone." That hardly fits with the idea that Jesus is seeking to be self-promoting. Also, Jesus tells the man to "offer for your cleansing what Moses commanded" but does not instruct the man to tell the priests how he became clean—no instructions to make mention of how Jesus healed him. We might assume that the former leper would explain this, but that doesn't seem to be the issue Jesus wants the man to pursue.

So, we're left with some questions. Why would Jesus want the former leper to show himself to the priests? Why make the prescribed offering? And what is the "witness" to the priests? If we think in terms of what is best for the former leper (rather than thinking that Jesus wants the man to do this in order to promote Himself), there might be an answer to these questions.

Leprosy rendered the afflicted not only sick but also ceremonially unclean. The only way for a leper to be reinstated into the community and received back as clean was to obtain a pronouncement of cleanliness from the priests.[37] The man knew he was clean and healed; Jesus knew it as well. But if the man had headed into the crowds announcing his healing without having been pronounced clean by the priests, he would still have been an outcast. Self-pronounced cleansing was not sufficient.

This is not busywork. Jesus is not assigning some random work for the former leper. Nor was Jesus looking for some good "press" from what He had done for the man. These instructions are for the former leper's benefit. Apart from taking these steps, he could not be restored and welcomed back into the community. Recognizing that, we can now answer why Jesus might have offered the man these instructions.

Jesus cares about more than merely performing the miracle, about more than a healing. As we've seen—and it's confirmed here—Jesus cares about the man. Jesus is personal and attentive to this man, not just his need for healing. Jesus is not merely "doing healing stuff," but He is addressing the man's whole life situation. Jesus is attentively caring for this man, not only bringing healing in a perfunctory way. Jesus addresses the man's physical need, but He also intends to bring healing and restoration to his entire life.

GETTING OUR HANDS ON THE RIGHT PIECES

Having looked carefully at the entire story, perhaps we can now recognize the most important pieces necessary for constructing the view of Jesus that Mark wants us to see. And seeing that, we might have some fresh insight for our own journeys with Jesus.

We have caught a glimpse of how those with only a small knowledge of Jesus seemed willing, nevertheless, to take risks with Him. And as we watch Jesus interacting with the leper, we can begin to understand why.

From the moment the leper approached Jesus, Jesus engages him in a purposeful and caring way. The man is not a problem to be dealt with or an illness to be treated—he is a person. Jesus feels deeply for the man, intentionally getting "up close and personal." Jesus cares deeply about the man's whole life and not merely the resolution of his immediate need for physical healing.

This attentive, caring, personal, engaged, purposeful, and willing Jesus is the Jesus that those who first met Him came to see. This is why they felt safe risking themselves with Him. Seeing Him this way—because this is who He is—can encourage us to bring our needs to Him, to take risks with Him, and to see what He might do about what troubles us.

You can risk with this Jesus. He is willing to engage you. He will stretch out His hand, His love, and His care to touch your life. He will advise and counsel you for your good. This is what He is like!

REFLECTING ON THIS TRUTH

FOR PERSONAL REFLECTION:

1. It seems to be common to imagine Jesus to be like the CEO of a big corporation—driven, focused on the job, a bit too busy to make a personal connection with someone low on the totem pole like me. But Jesus is not like this. As you let this snapshot of Jesus help shape how you think about Him, talk with Him—about His attentiveness, His personal care, His compassion, and His willingness to get up close and personal with you.

2. What needs or concerns or troubles have you been holding back from sharing with Jesus? What is keeping you from risking bringing those issues to Him? Seeing Jesus as presented here, take a deep breath, look to Him, and begin to speak to Him about those issues.

3. The leper was desperate. Knowing what he did about Jesus and realizing the hopeless and complex situation he was facing, he begged Jesus for help. That is a great attitude to have when we come to Jesus with our needs. When I come to Jesus as if He is just one possible option among others for dealing with my situation, I may be setting things up in such a way that He won't respond. Abandon yourself to Him—He is good enough, kind enough, personal enough, and gracious enough to warrant that abandonment.

FOR GROUP DISCUSSION:

1. What do you think Simon and Andrew saw in Jesus that might have encouraged them to mention their mother's illness to Him? Without any certainty that He could or would heal her, what might have been going on in their hearts?

2. What do you think would have been going through the minds and hearts of those who brought their sick and oppressed friends to Simon's mother-in-law's house? What might their expectations have been based on?

3. The crowd took risks with Jesus. The leper took a risk with Jesus. Knowing relatively little about Jesus, what justified their taking such risks? Does your understanding of Jesus open you to take risks with Him? Is there a risk He is currently asking you to take?

CHAPTER FOUR

JUST A MOMENT, PLEASE

JAIRUS' DAUGHTER AND THE BLEEDING WOMAN

But the woman fearing and trembling, aware of what had happened to her, came and fell down before Him, and told Him the whole truth.

—Mark 5:33

IF YOU'VE HAD THE OPPORTUNITY to flip through a friend's photo album of their last vacation or favorite trip, it will be clear that some of the photos have more of a story than others. Although you might not see a great deal of difference between the photos—there's your friend in front of big building, that's him in front of a rock, that's her in front of a bunch of rocks—some of the photos are special.

It's easy to tell which ones. If the person who took the photographs is leafing through the album with you, he might pause just a bit longer on a certain snapshot before turning the page. She might even touch the picture, hesitating before going on. If the album owner is narrating as you leaf through the pictures, it's even more obvious which pictures have special meaning. You can tell. They are the photos he or she takes time to explain to you, often in great detail.

"Now I know that this just looks like a pile of rocks, but it was here that . . ." And before long, you realize that there is more to that snapshot than you first imagined.

Something similar occurs in the Gospels. As Matthew, Mark, John, or Luke wrote what the Spirit wanted them to record about the life and ministry of Jesus, they lingered over some of the pictures. In this way the Spirit calls attention to certain facets of Jesus' life and ministry.

Seeing as Matthew and John were eyewitnesses to these events, their more elaborate telling of a particular event or moment may be due, in part, to the personal impact that event had on them. It is believed that Mark wrote his Gospel based on the reminiscences of Peter. When Mark dwells on some particular facet of the life and ministry of Jesus it may well be that that moment had significant impact on Peter's life.

Because of two ideas—that the lingering is part of the Spirit's design and that the lingering may be rooted in the impact the moment had on the writers—when one of the Gospel writers dwells on a miracle, giving us details beyond the minimal report of the healing, we would do well to pay attention. There is something here, something more than meets the eye at first glance.

If we look carefully, we might discover what exactly made such an impact on Jesus' first followers and friends.

AN INTERRUPTION ON THE WAY

Let's turn our attention to just one such an account. A number of the Gospel writers record it, but we will follow Mark's report. As Mark tells us, Jesus' ministry has been growing. He has touched and healed and delivered many. Sometimes, Mark just gives us the headline version: "Jesus healed many . . ." (Mark 1:34). But then, we come to this account, where Mark weaves two fascinating miracles together.

> And when Jesus had crossed over again in the boat to the other side, a great multitude gathered about Him; and He stayed by the seashore. And one of the synagogue officials named Jairus came up, and upon seeing Him, fell at His feet, and entreated Him earnestly, saying, "My little daughter is at the point of death; please come and lay Your hands on her, that she may get well and live." And He went off with him; and a great multitude was following Him and pressing in on Him.
>
> And a woman who had had a hemorrhage for twelve years, and had endured much at the hands of many physicians, and had spent all that she had and was not helped at all, but rather had grown worse, after hearing about Jesus, came up in the crowd behind Him, and touched His cloak. For she thought, "If I just touch His garments, I shall get well."
>
> And immediately the flow of her blood was dried up; and she felt in her body that she was healed of her affliction. And

immediately Jesus, perceiving in Himself that the power proceeding from Him had gone forth, turned around in the crowd and said, "Who touched My garments?"

And His disciples said to Him, "You see the multitude pressing in on You, and You say, 'Who touched Me?'"

And He looked around to see the woman who had done this. But the woman fearing and trembling, aware of what had happened to her, came and fell down before Him, and told Him the whole truth. And He said to her, "Daughter, your faith has made you well; go in peace, and be healed of your affliction."

While He was still speaking, they came from the house of the synagogue official, saying, "Your daughter has died, why trouble the Teacher any more?"

But Jesus, overhearing what was being spoken, said to the synagogue official, "Do not be afraid any longer, only believe." And He allowed no one to follow with Him, expect Peter and James and John and the brother of James.

And they came to the house of the synagogue official; and He beheld a commotion, and people loudly weeping and wailing. And entering in, He said to them, "Why make a commotion and weep? The child has not died, but is asleep."

> And they were laughing at Him. But putting them all out, He took along the child's father and mother and His own companions, and entered the room where the child was. And taking the child by the hand, He said to her, "Talitha kum!" (which translated means, "Little girl, I say to you, arise!").
>
> And immediately the girl got up and began to walk; for she was twelve years old. And immediately they were completely astounded. And He gave them strict orders that no one should know about this; and He said that something should be given to her to eat.
>
> —Mark 5:21–43

One of the things that make this particular miracle story so intriguing is the way two separate miracles are woven together. Jesus begins to head one way, and then it looks like He gets sidetracked and attends to something else. Walking through the details of this account will help us pick up on particularly fascinating insights into Jesus.

Apparently, this synagogue official[38] has heard something about Jesus. Given the critical situation he is facing, he has heard enough to lead him to one he thinks can help. It's not clear exactly what he anticipates Jesus might do, but clearly he is of the mind that if Jesus were to only show up at his house, his little girl[39] wouldn't end up dead.

With this request, Jesus heads off, promptly going with the man. However, they are not going to the man's home alone, seeing as the crowd kept on following. The man came, Jesus heard, and the Jesus and the crowd take a new heading.

From every indication, Jesus was intending to go along with the synagogue official. We can conclude that the official must have been both feeling a great sense of urgency (his daughter is at "the point of death") and a great sense of hope (since Jesus consents to go with him). We do not know how far the man traveled to get to Jesus, but we can be certain that this man is counting every step as they head home, hurrying Jesus along as much as he thinks he can without showing disrespect.

And then it happens. Jesus stops. He turns around. The synagogue official is a step or two ahead now . . . and he turns to find Jesus . . . He's not there! He was right beside him a moment ago, but now? Then he sees Him.

Jesus has stopped. He is asking something of the crowd. Even the disciples seem to think the question is strange. He is looking into the mass of humanity that has been pressing in on Him, inquiring as to which of them touched[40] Him. He is not upset about it, but He does seem insistent. Apparently something has happened. Jesus is committed to pursuing the matter.

Don't you think the synagogue official may have gently pulled on His robe? "We need to go; my daughter is dying." Don't you think this father, who had earnestly pled with Jesus just moments before, would have been troubled that Jesus has stopped? "We can come back later—after my daughter is well!"

But Jesus stays where He is and waits for someone to come forward in response to His inquiry. Someone does. An older woman. And she speaks.

She explains that He must be looking for her, for she knows something has happened to her. She has felt it in her body. She knows she is healed. She is smiling. Jesus is smiling, too. But the father of the soon-to-be-dead child is not. He is puzzled.

Jesus begins to talk with her. She begins to talk with Him.[41]

WELL, FIRST THEY WHEELED ME INTO THE OPERATING ROOM

Have you ever been on the receiving end of a play-by-play description of a friend's recent surgery? Because it was so meaningful to him, because she endured so much and was so pleased with the outcome, the patient tends to rehearse every step along the way. What was a simple one-hour outpatient surgical procedure takes two hours to tell.

Often, those who have endured such an ordeal have a need to talk about it. Sometimes, the more traumatic the experience and the greater the need, the longer it will take for the retelling.

Jesus is speaking with a woman who has been through a great ordeal, and who has now come to the end of it. She is healed. She knows it. He knows it.[42] And because of that, she begins to tell Jesus.

She had been suffering with the affliction for twelve years. She has spent a great deal of time in poor health. And "she told Him the whole truth" about it.

She had been suffering with an affliction that rendered her spiritually unclean.[43] She has been an outcast from her family and community.[44] And "she told Him the whole truth" about it.

She had been to countless doctors looking for help and health. She found no help in any of the many different options she pursued. And "she told Him the whole truth" about it.

She had spent everything she had seeking some cure. She had not only been an unwelcome, unclean person, she was also in poverty. And "she told Him the whole truth" about it.

Twelve years of suffering. Left ritually unclean and unaccepted in the community of faith. Countless treatments and doctors. Spent all that she had. You do the math. How long did it take her to share her story? Two minutes? Ten minutes? An hour? More?

How long did it seem to be to the man who thought he'd never hold his little daughter in his arms again? How long did it seem to this father who was growing more convinced that he'd never see his little girl grow up to be a woman, a wife, and a mother?

What are we to make of this? What would you have been thinking if you were this father? I believe it's pretty clear.

"Jesus, the woman is healed. Her problem is over. She's okay. You don't have time to listen to her life's story. And my daughter is going to die!"

But Jesus waits, listens, and takes in every word as the woman tells Him the whole truth about all she has suffered.

Why does Jesus do this?

He is not wasting time. Jesus was always about His Father's business.[45] He isn't trying to figure out what happened. He already knows the woman is healed. He must be doing it because it is important . . . to the woman.

Here is a woman who has told her story, all she has suffered, to so many, without ever being able to come to any meaningful ending. The story never came to a happy conclusion. She was always writing another sad chapter. More suffering. More rejection. More loneliness. More expenditures. But she never got to share a happy ending. Until now.

It may just be that Jesus knows that for her health—for her full health—someone needs to hear her whole story, from the start all the way to the happy ending. So He stops. He listens. And did you notice? It is only after the woman has told Jesus her "whole story" that Jesus sends the woman away in peace. This suggests that the conversation Jesus had with her was essential for her.

I CAN SPARE . . .

As will be clear in so many of the accounts we explore, Jesus deals with people as individuals. That is surely part of what is going on here. It's not enough for Jesus merely to know that the woman has been healed. He wants her healing to be complete; He wants her life, her soul, and her heart to be restored as well. So He takes the time to let her tell Him all about it.

What do I see here? It isn't simply that Jesus treats people as individuals, as real persons; that's true. But I think the other thing I see here is that Jesus has all the time necessary—He takes all the time needed—to respond deeply and fully to this woman.

I have been in all too many doctor's offices when, just as I have begun to explain what I'm feeling and why I'm there, the doctor nods, pulls out his prescription pad, and tells me he knows what I've got and if I just take two of these twice a day, I'll be fine.

And you know, I usually do get better. But I didn't feel that the doctor had time for me.

I have stood in line at too many service station counters trying to find someone who will let me explain the noise and the "feeling" I have when I've been driving my car, only to be told that they're really backed up, but if I'd care to leave it someone will look at it. And they usually do take a look and, after paying for the adjustment of some part I don't know I could spell, the car does seem to drive better. But I didn't feel that the mechanic had time for me.

I have even been in churches where I have come to build relationships and where I am just beginning to learn to open up and risk with someone, and as I am trying . . . slowly . . . carefully . . . to let someone have a peek at what's going on inside of me, the meeting is over, prayers are said, and we break for "fellowship" around the food in the next room. And the praying usually does make a difference. But I didn't feel that my brothers and sisters really had time for me.

But Jesus does! I see it here. The woman was healed. The heart of the problem was solved. But the problem of the heart needed some additional time. And Jesus stopped, long enough, even in the midst of such a serious task He was on, to give this unknown woman all the time she needed.

He was not too busy to listen . . . all the way . . . to what she needed to share with Him.

MEANWHILE, BACK AT THE RANCH

But let's not forget: there is another story woven into that of the woman with the flow of blood. Standing right next to her, listening to her as Jesus patiently hears it all, is the man whose daughter is on the brink of death. The moment it is clear that Jesus has given the woman all the attention He intends to give her, the father and his new Friend are off at a quick pace for the home, and the sick bed and, hopefully, a little daughter who is still breathing.

But what do we find as Jairus hurries Jesus along, once again?

It is too late! The report comes. The little girl has died. The father's worst fears have come true. The delay was too long. The side trip was not a shortcut. The time wasted listening to the woman has taken its toll on his child. She is dead.

At that moment, Jesus speaks a simple word to the anxious father: "Do not be afraid any longer, only believe." Obviously this father has been devastated by the news. Yet Jesus has a word for him. "Do not continue being afraid about what is going to happen. Just trust Me."[46]

Apparently, Jairus does, in some clear way, trust Jesus. He doesn't send Jesus back. He doesn't throw up his hands and declare all further efforts fruitless. Jesus intends to go all the way to Jairus' house with him, and Jairus apparently willingly brought him along. He must be trusting Jesus—trusting Him, His advice, His direction, His intentions—regardless of how things may seem to Jairus at the moment. But things don't look good!

When they arrive at the house, it becomes clear. The little girl has been dead for a while. The mourners are already there. The word has spread. The mourning clothes are arranged and those who know have come to weep with the family. They took too long. Jesus' delay was fatal.

But Jesus is not finished. He speaks another word. He addresses the mourners. "She's not dead. She's only asleep." They laugh. As if they can't tell a dead child when they see one! As if they could be so easily fooled! They had held vigil for some time. They all had feared the worse. And it came. When the father was gone. It's over now.

But Jesus is not yet through. He puts the mourners out. He takes the family—mother and father—and a few of His closest friends into the little girl's room. He pauses, He steps forward, He reaches for her, and He speaks. "Little girl,[47] I say to you, arise!"

And she does! Something incredible has happened. She not only sits up. She's immediately up and around; she is fully restored. She has been raised from the dead!

Jesus, ever attentive to the personal needs of those He cares for, instructs the parents to make sure she has something to eat. How like Him. She is fully well, but she may be hungry. He wants to make sure that in the commotion of her resurrection such a simple thing isn't overlooked.

What is it that we see in Jesus, here in the house of this synagogue official?

We see, again, that He treats those who come to Him with needs as individuals. He cares for this little girl, and not just as a "case of resurrection." He tenderly attends to her fully. But, again, there is something more.

IT'S ABOUT TIME

It was His timing. It was perfect. No, He didn't get there when the official had hoped. No, He didn't arrive in time to stop what they had feared. No, His timing wasn't really what they had thought it should be. But He wasn't too late. He never is.

I believe this is one of the threads that hold these two accounts together.[48] They both illustrate different facets of the same truth about our great Friend and Savior: His timing is perfect. He never dawdles unnecessarily. He never delays beyond the time in which He is able to work. He never is too busy with one thing to keep from spending time on another needing attention. He has all the time in the world to do all that He intends on doing.

He is never hurried, rushed, short, or too busy for us. He is never overbooked, overworked, or out of time. He is never running behind schedule, nor will you find His time with you squeezed out by other demands. You see, in both these stories, Jesus was in control of the time. He took the time needed for the woman with the flow of blood in spite of what seemed like an overwhelmingly urgent need. He had plenty of time to attend to the little girl after spending all the time He needed in doing what might have appeared to some as trivial.

We live in a world that appears to have some kind of disease when it comes to time. With all the "conveniences" we have, we still never seem to have enough time. We live hectic lives: wired, connected, in touch, but still out of time. When the end of the day comes, all too often we fall exhausted into bed. The list of what should have been done (if only there had been enough time) looms ominous and large. The next morning finds us trying to get up when the alarm cries out it's morning greeting, knowing that this day, too, will be a mad dash to try to find enough time to do what we think must be done. We just never seem to have time for what really matters.

That is one of the reasons why I love this episode from the life of Jesus. I find this to be a powerful picture of Jesus. In a world where we so often don't seem to have time to get done what we feel must get done, He does.

All too often I go through my day, coming to the end of seemingly endless demands, feeling as if I do not have the time I need to do what is most important. The urgent, the noisiest, the most-burdensome things may get done, but there are times when the things that I really feel are the most important things in life don't get attention. I just don't feel I have enough time.

But Jesus does. He has enough time to do what must be done, what has to be done. He has enough time, and He takes the time to do what is essential. No more and no less. He does not waste time or squander it. He does not show up a minute late and a dollar short. He is on time in all He does and takes the time He needs to do all He needs to do.

How I need to see this picture of Him. I need to know that this is true about Him.

Even in my walk with Him I feel that time is a problem. He doesn't seem to answer my prayers according to my calendar. He doesn't always resolve the things weighing on me on my timetable. Sometimes, I feel as if the day is so busy that He and I just won't be able to get any time together at all.

But time is not a problem for Him.

He answers every prayer at just the right time.

He meets our needs at the most opportune moment.

And whenever I turn to speak with Him, to hear from Him, or to lean on Him, He always has all the time I need.

He had enough time for the woman with her need. But He still didn't run out of time to address the concerns of an anxious father. He took all the time necessary to meet the woman's need and still was not rushed or late or tragically delayed in helping a little girl in her moment of great need.

What could be better than walking, hand in hand throughout your day, with One whose timing is so impeccable. Why not do that? Just reach up, take hold of His hand, and tell Him that you're glad to trust His timing.

REFLECTING ON THIS TRUTH

FOR PERSONAL REFLECTION:

1. When was the last time you really had time alone with Jesus? Do you feel that you just don't have the time to spend? Jesus can and will meet with you at any hour of any day. Whenever you need Him to be there, He has time for you. Ask Him to show you where, in the midst of your day, you might be able to get that time with Him.

2. Have you ever felt that Jesus just didn't do what you needed Him to do, when you felt it needed to be done? When that happens (and it does!), it's easy to feel disappointed; to feel frustrated in Jesus and His timing. And what often happens after is that we stop talking with Him; we don't want to feel that disappointment

again. But, you see, His timing is perfect. And that's not just a cliché. He really does do what needs to be done when it needs to be done. So, if you've been holding back from talking with Him because of a disappointment, get back together with Him. Admit to Him that His timing is best; that He really does know. And get back in step with the One who is always on time.

FOR GROUP DISCUSSION:

1. How does watching the way Jesus ministers in a "timely" fashion impact the way you think of what He is doing in your life? In the lives of those with whom you share life?

2. If we really believed that Jesus' timing was perfect—that He was never early and never late—how could we better encourage one another in trusting Him?

3. What would it take for us to live the way Jesus does: within time constraints and without facing challenges about time? How could we live less rushed lives and yet still have time for what really was important?

CHAPTER FIVE

MORE THAN ANTICIPATED

THE RESTORATION OF THE PARALYZED MAN

And [the man] got up and immediately picked up the pallet and went out in the sight of everyone, so that they were all amazed and were glorifying God.

—Mark 2:12a

SOMETIMES IT IS A RELATIVELY simple thing. You purchase a new cell phone—the old one having breathed its last. You weren't looking for anything fancy. Just something to replace the one that no longer lets you call anyone who has a seven in their phone number and that no longer lets you send a text message with r's or s's. So you settle for the new model the salesman in the store said would serve your needs.

But you got more than you thought. The new phone does things you didn't even think about doing with a phone. GPS and multiple "apps." When you purchased the phone you didn't even know what an "app" was, but after a few months you can't imagine how you managed without such features.

Initially, you didn't realize the possible benefits of a new phone. Now the new phone has changed so much of how you do life. You got more than you anticipated.

This happens when people encounter Jesus. Someone approaches Jesus with a need, some obvious concern. As we watch Jesus touch the person, it becomes clear that those who come to Him with some need often end up with more than they anticipated. There is often much more going on than underscored by those "headlines" in your Bible.[49]

If we don't read the accounts found in the Gospels attentively, though, we could end up skipping over some of that "more." We watch Jesus heal someone of a physical affliction or deliver someone from oppression. Without appropriate attentiveness, we end up drawing an identical conclusion from every healing and every time He delivers someone oppressed: Jesus does amazing things. Although that is true, there is more we could see.

Jesus doesn't, typically, simply meet the obvious need. He does so much more. As we begin to see this, we gain a fresh perspective on the sort of man Jesus is.

HOME IS WHERE YOU . . . [50]

In order to understand something of this next miracle, it will be helpful to get a running start. We need to get into the flow of the story Mark is telling.

In Mark's account, Jesus' public ministry began in Capernaum. Having gathered a few men to travel with Him (Mark 1:16–20), He entered the synagogue in that city and on the Sabbath began to teach (1:21–22). As He taught, a demonized man cried out, and Jesus delivered the man from his torment (1:23–28).

Leaving the synagogue, Jesus entered Simon's mother-in-law's house. Because she was suffering from a fever, Simon told Jesus about her and He healed her (1:29–31). As word of that healing spread in the city—and after the Sabbath was over—other sick and infirm showed up at Simon's mother-in-law's house where Jesus proceeded to minister to those in need (1:32–34).

As we saw in an earlier chapter, a surprising turn comes as Jesus decides early the next morning to leave and go into neighboring cities (1:35–39). More ministry follows, Mark giving us a synopsis of what was happening.

But then Jesus does return home.

> When He had come back to Capernaum several days afterward, it was heard that He was at home. And many were gathered together, so that there was no longer room, not ever near the door; and He was speaking the word to them.
>
> —Mark 2:1–2

When Mark refers to Jesus being "at home," this doesn't necessarily mean that Jesus owned a house in Capernaum. The language might only be indicating that Jesus was at the house He frequented—perhaps Simon's mother-in-law's residence. Her home had been the sight of Jesus' previous ministry in the city and would be a likely "home base" for Him when He returned to Capernaum.

After Jesus had settled in there, a crowd showed up. That they were there is hardly surprising seeing that when Jesus had departed Capernaum earlier, many were looking for Him—presumably to have their needs met (Mark 1:37). There is, initially, no particular mention of Jesus extending healing and bringing deliverance on this occasion; He is speaking with the crowd.

Use your "sanctified imagination" to picture this real situation described by Mark. Imagine what it might have been like at that house.

How many people were there? More than a few; a large crowd. What are they doing? Where are they all? Even the door is blocked because of the crush of people. People are straining to see, to hear, to experience something because Jesus is there. Then something quite surprising happens.

CAN WE COME IN?

Although Mark doesn't tell us that any of those packed into the house were there to be healed, it could be that some had come for that reason. Such a situation would not be unusual, given what happened the last time Jesus was in Capernaum and knowing that when He left some were still looking to Him for ministry. Mark, however, does tell us about one person in need of healing.

> And they came, bringing to Him a paralytic, carried by four men. Being unable to get to Him because of the crowd, they removed the roof above Him; and when they had dug an opening, they let down the pallet on which the paralytic was lying. And Jesus seeing their

> faith said to the paralytic, "Son, your sins are forgiven." But some of the scribes were sitting there and reasoning in their hearts, "Why does this man speak that way? He is blaspheming; who can forgive sins but God alone?" Immediately Jesus, aware in His spirit that they were reasoning that way within themselves, said to them, "Why are you reasoning about these things in your hearts? Which is easier, to say to the paralytic, 'Your sins are forgiven'; or to say, 'Get up, and pick up your pallet and walk'? But so that you may know that the Son of Man has authority on earth to forgive sins"—He said to the paralytic, "I say to you, get up, pick up your pallet and go home." And he got up and immediately picked up the pallet and went out in the sight of everyone, so that they were all amazed and were glorifying God, saying, "We have never seen anything like this."
>
> —Mark 2:3–12

Whatever is going on here, Mark has his eyes on more than the paralyzed man. Although that man is key to the moment, there are two groups of people that also appear to be in view: the four friends and the scribes. What can we learn about Jesus from these three participants in the story?

Let's start with the simplest one—the paralyzed man. What do we know about him? When we first meet him, he can do nothing for himself. When we reach the end of the account, he can walk out. The initial conclusion is that the passage shows us that Jesus can heal—not an insignificant thought, but a bit superficial seeing Mark has already made that clear for his readers. In this story, there are two other things Mark tells us about this man.

First, the man apparently also had a "soul need." He clearly needed the physical healing Jesus offered him. But he also must have needed the spiritual healing Jesus brought to him in forgiving his sins. (We'll explore the significance of that in a moment.)

There is no indication in this text that there was any connection between the man's physical affliction and his spiritual need.[51] But that Jesus addressed both issues should not be overlooked.

CAN YOU DO SOMETHING ABOUT . . . ?

As the man was being lowered in front of Jesus, one of his needs was blatant; the other, not nearly so. But as we have seen,[52] Jesus deals with those who come to him as whole people, addressing more than merely the obvious problem. For Jesus to deal with the man's internal need as well as his external need is consistent with what we have seen—and a helpful reminder of Jesus' desire to care for us in similar ways.

When we come to Jesus with our obvious and external need—whatever it might be—in addressing that need He may also speak to something else in our lives. In His kindness, He might bring physical healing and then ask us about a matter of the heart. He could bring a change in a relationship, and then also call our attention to some internal struggle that is hindering our ministering in His love to others. He could provide resources for some tangible need and subsequently call our attention to particular priorities He wants to address. Jesus desires to deal with us in such full and complete ways.

But in this case, there is a bit more beyond just the healing—both physical and spiritual. What happens when Jesus healed the man? When his paralysis is relieved? "He got up and immediately picked up the pallet and went out in the sight of everyone."

For many years, I had a quadriplegic friend; he had been paralyzed in a swimming accident. Thinking about Jesus' healing of the paralyzed man in this account, I cannot help but think about my friend.

If Jesus were to bring healing to my friend, it would take a great deal more than the alleviation of his paralysis for him to stand up and keep his balance, let alone pick up any load and carry it. My friend's unused muscles had atrophied; it took some doing even to help him into a t-shirt because of the loss of mobility in his arms. Sometimes just helping my friend sit up could present a challenge. Seeing as he was reclined for so much of the day, the upright position could put a strain on his circulatory system.

Recognizing these factors, I am forced to reflect on what happened in this account. Jesus must have done so much more than merely solve this man's paralysis problem. Muscles had to be restored. The man's circulatory system would have to have been "upgraded." A sense of balance must have been "downloaded" for him to be able to stand and walk. Unused strength would have to be revitalized.

The formerly paralyzed man got an incredible gift—a gift that included not only the healing of his paralysis but a remarkable restoration of vitality and vigor, as well as the resolution of his sin problem.

HAVE YOU FORGOTTEN SOMETHING?

But the paralyzed man is not the only character in Mark's account. Mark also tells us about four men. What do we know about them? Not a great deal—but there are a few significant pieces.

> And they came, bringing to Him a paralytic, carried by four men. Being unable to get to Him because of the crowd, they removed the roof above Him; and when they had dug an opening, they let down the pallet on which the paralytic was lying. And Jesus seeing their faith said to the paralytic, "Son, your sins are forgiven."
>
> —Mark 2:3–5

These four men are good friends. Clearly, their paralyzed acquaintance could not have made his way, by himself, to see Jesus. So they arranged to bring him. We do not know whether the paralyzed man wanted this, but we do know that the four friends wanted this.

When drawing close to the house where they knew Jesus was, how do you think they must have felt when they found their way blocked by a large crowd? With people pressing in all around and the doorway blocked, what might have gone through their minds? "I guess the plan is off. There's no way to get to Jesus now. We'll have to wait for another chance." But apparently this is not what they concluded.

Mark's description is quite specific.

"They removed the roof above Him." Mark's expression means they "unroofed the roof." It's easy to imagine what these four men did. A roof made of wood or tiles of clay and mortar; covered over with some rain-repellent thatch. To start, they would have had to remove the first layer—unroofing the roof.

"They . . . dug an opening." That's a pretty aggressive picture. These four men had to dig an opening—that's right, like taking shovels to the ground or picks to rock. Breaking up the solid part of the roof, they made an opening that would have accommodated the bed on which their friend was lying.

What would have been going on inside the house while these four crazed friends were having a workday on the roof? Pieces begin to fall in—obviously all the pieces wouldn't have stayed on the roof. Debris, noise, dust, stone, splinters. It must have continued for a least a short while until a rather substantial hole was opened. The dust only began to settle when the four began lowering down the bed on which their paralyzed friend was confined.

"And Jesus seeing their faith . . ." What can this mean? Of course, we might read our developed theological thinking about Jesus back into this account and assume that Jesus, with divine insight, saw into their souls and recognized in them some basic faith.[53] But the way that Mark tells the story, it might be that Jesus saw their activity and, having seen that, recognized it as faith.[54]

This early-in-the-Gospel picture of faith illustrates something for us.[55] There are only a dozen and half mentions of "faith" or "believing" in Mark; this passage provides a great opportunity to reflect on what faith looks like.

What do you see in these four? What is pictured?

Perhaps what we see here is the four men being "all in." These four men are desperate to get help for their friend. They are committed to doing all they can to get their friend before Jesus. They take risks; they give themselves without reservation; and they are wholly dependent upon Jesus and what He might do. They abandon themselves to this Man (a man they likely know far less about than do you or I).

That gives us a starting point for understanding faith. Faith looks like radical abandonment to Jesus—because we see Him to be the only one who might be able to do something about our situation.

So, there they are. Dust covered, panting hard, trying to think through how they will explain their actions to the owner of the house they have just deconstructed, lowering their friend hand-over-hand. They are doing that because they see it as their one option. And then they hear Jesus speak: "Son, your sins are forgiven."

I wonder how the four men might have responded to this statement. Did they just stop in mid-lowering? Did the four look with startled glances at one another? Did they say something? "Sins!? We weren't thinking about forgiveness. We want our friend to walk! What are you doing, Jesus? Haven't you forgotten something? Our friend is paralyzed!"

Could they hear the conversation going on between Jesus and the religious leaders in the room? Perhaps. Did they understand the question being raised by the religious leaders? Perhaps. Did they have to wait very long for what they wanted for their friend in the first place? Probably not long at all.

My opinion is that Jesus was not "fooling around" in speaking to the paralyzed man's sin problem; I believe Jesus intended fully to heal the man from the start. He just chose to start with the sin problem. So the four did get what they wanted for their friend. They just got more than they anticipated.

Whatever the formerly paralyzed man had expected, it may be that Jesus exceeded his expectations as well. The friend of the four men walked out of the house—healed, restored, forgiven. In a real sense, this formerly paralyzed man was given an entirely new life—a gift that came only because his friends sought to get him in front of Jesus. And they all got more than expected.

EXCUSE ME! WHAT DO YOU THINK YOU'RE DOING?

There is one more facet of this encounter that still requires some attention—the exchange He has with the religious leaders. Mark identifies them as "scribes." Scribes were those responsible for the copying and preservation of the Old Testament text. As such, they were very familiar with the words of the Scriptures and were often looked to as those who could resolve questions or expound on the texts.

Jesus' first words to the paralyzed man were, "Your sins are forgiven you." This remark provoked thought in the scribes. "But some of the scribes were sitting there and reasoning in their hearts, 'Why does this man speak that way? He is blaspheming; who can forgive sins but God alone?'"

Why did the scribes respond this way? Some hear their words as if they were saying that for Jesus to speak a word of forgiveness to the man He must have been making a direct divine claim. It is true that the scribes were raising the question of blasphemy and insisting that only God can forgive sins. But we need to think carefully about their concern.

We don't speak of blasphemy much these days; in fact even in the New Testament it is only mentioned a few times.[56] At the heart of the idea of blasphemy is to speak in a purposefully disparaging way about God—to intentionally defame Him. But why would the scribes raise this question on the basis of Jesus' pronouncement that the man's sins were forgiven?

God gave the Old Testament sacrificial system; the priesthood and Temple practices found their origins in the Scriptures. Part of those divinely revealed instructions included addressing the sin problem. Numerous sacrifices specifically dealt with the forgiveness of sins.[57] Recognizing that, it would be proper to insist that only God could forgive sin—seeing as sin is an offense against God and seeing that He had ordained a specific way to deal with sin.

With that understanding, we might get some perspective about what troubled the scribes. It may not have been that they were shocked because they thought Jesus was "claiming to be God." They might have responded the way they did because they assumed that God's only ordained way of extending forgiveness was through the priests and by way of the sacrificial system. Jesus' offer of forgiveness apart from the priesthood and the sacrifices would be perceived as circumventing what God had instituted. He could readily be perceived to be taking God lightly and disparaging His accepted means of providing forgiveness. In this way, to their way of thinking, Jesus would be blaspheming.

This approach to the scribes' concern seems justified by the way Jesus responds. If the charge of blasphemy was linked to Jesus making a direct divine claim, it is surprising that Jesus didn't respond to that—He doesn't assert, "I can forgive sin because I am the divine second person of the Godhead come to earth." Jesus' response points in a different direction.

Jesus wanted the scribes to know that He, "the Son of Man," "has authority on earth to forgive sins." Listen carefully to His words. He identifies Himself as "the Son of Man." Although we might hear that title as one with a divine ring to it, it is a title that would have been used to refer to the Messiah—God's appointed and anointed deliverer.[58] By itself, it would not have been heard as claiming, "I am God."

Jesus as "the Son of Man" affirms His authority on earth to forgive sins. To speak of authority doesn't necessarily convey the idea of divine right.[59] Jesus is affirming that, as the Son of Man, He has delegated authority—God-given permission—to extend forgiveness. But that is not significantly different than what the priests themselves did in Jesus' day—they had God-given permission, as priests, to extend God's forgiveness. The scribes' problem seemed to be that Jesus was approaching forgiveness outside of the prevailing pattern.

But even that should not have been entirely inconceivable to them. In the Old Testament, forgiveness from God was, at times, extended apart from the priests, apart from the sacrificial system. Nathan, the prophet, extended God's forgiveness to David after his sin with Bathsheba, without recourse to priests or sacrifice (2 Samuel 12:13).

Jesus graciously addressed the scribes' question. Although His words might sound a bit cryptic, Jesus was creating a bridge for them to think with Him.

> Immediately Jesus, aware in His spirit that they were reasoning that way within themselves, said to them, "Why are you reasoning about these things in your hearts? Which is easier, to say to the paralytic, 'Your sins are forgiven'; or to say, 'Get up, and pick up your pallet and walk'? But so that you may know that the Son of Man has authority on earth to forgive sins" — He said to the paralytic, "I say to you, get up, pick up your pallet and go home."
>
> —Mark 2:8–11

THINK WITH ME

At first read, we might conclude the harder thing to *do* is to forgive sins; and, of course, that is a more significant spiritual issue. But it is easier to *say* to someone "your sins are forgiven" than to *say,* "you are healed of your affliction." The words of forgiveness have no evidential proof; therefore, it would be easier to pronounce forgiveness. The words of healing would have to be backed up with demonstrative power; therefore, it is harder to pronounce healing.

Jesus' reasoning seems to be clear. He is inviting the scribes to do some honest reflection. If He can demonstrate that He has authority—the delegated right—to speak a word of physical healing to a paralyzed man, might He not also have authority—the delegated right—to extend forgiveness?

Jesus follows up His provision of spiritual restoration with the provision of physical healing.

> And [the man] got up and immediately picked up the pallet and went out in the sight of everyone, so that they were all amazed and were glorifying God, saying, "We have never seen anything like this."
>
> —Mark 2:12

Remarkable. Mark apparently wants us to know that even the scribes were counted among the "all"—"they were *all* amazed and were glorifying God, saying, 'We have never seen anything like this.'"

They were amazed.[60] That means that they were staggered by what they saw and experienced. And they glorified God. They apparently understood that God was, somehow, responsible for what had happened, and they appropriately responded in a worshipful way.

But this means they got more than they had expected.

Did you notice? The scribes had only raised the question "in their hearts." They hadn't ventured to ask Jesus their question. However, Jesus graciously addressed their concern without betraying to the crowd what they were reasoning about in their own minds. Seeing as they had not asked their question out loud, it was unlikely the scribes anticipated receiving an answer. But Jesus offered them one.

They longed to understand how it could be that a man could extend forgiveness for sin. But they only internally wrestled with the idea. However, Jesus offered them more. They were drawn to see that, perhaps, this Man did have God-given authority to forgive sin. They were given a reason to believe that God was extending grace and healing and forgiveness through this Man. They went from raising the question of blasphemy to responding in praise to God.

Why were these scribes there, in the house, listening as Jesus taught? Mark does not tell us. Perhaps they were curious about Jesus and His teaching. Maybe they were puzzled by what they had heard about Him. From the questions in their heart, it's clear they were not yet sure what to make of Him. I seriously doubt they anticipated the outcome when they first saw the paralyzed man being lowered through the ceiling.

EVERYBODY GETS SOMETHING

In the end, each of the participants in this account received more than anticipated. The paralyzed man could hardly have imagined where his life would have ended up after an encounter with Jesus—healed, restored and revitalized, forgiven, and given an entirely new life. The four friends likely had not anticipated all that Jesus would do for their friend—their desperate reaching for healing grace ended up ushering in such rich blessings. The scribes could not have predetermined in their minds and hearts what would happen when they sat down to listen to this compelling teacher—their small amount of curiosity resulted both in challenges to their thinking and in a heart-response of worship.

And in each case, Jesus is the reason for the "more than anticipated."

Jesus has healed people before . . . but without extending forgiveness as He does here. Jesus has ministered to the needs of people who have been brought to Him . . . yet never quite as dramatically and whole-life-changing as happened with the friend of these four men. Jesus has taught and explained Himself . . . but without building such a clear bridge between Himself and those who struggled with Him. In each case, this encounter with Jesus left the participants with more than they could have anticipated.

If, when we come to Jesus with a need, He meets only the need we present, only responds as we expect Him to respond, and fails to address the questions with which we secretly wrestle within our own souls, all too often we would leave with huge needs still unmet.

But Jesus does not wait for me to be fully aware of all that I might need. Jesus does not need for me clearly to articulate everything that is weighing on me. Jesus isn't put off when I don't know how or don't have the courage to ask those nagging questions that keep me at a distance from Him.

As we approach Jesus, He sees. He sees everything we need. He knows what must happen, even if it goes beyond what we consider important. He is cognizant of the questions that need answers for us to move toward Him rather than pull away from Him, even if we struggle to articulate such questions.

Jesus consistently does more than we can anticipate . . . and we need Him to.

Paul captures this idea well, in the way he speaks of God's gracious work on our behalf:

> Now to Him who is able to do far more abundantly beyond all that we ask or think, according to the power

> that works within us, to Him be the glory . . . forever and ever. Amen.
>
> —Ephesians 3:20–21

REFLECTING ON THIS TRUTH

FOR PERSONAL REFLECTION:

1. It's easy to be selective in how we approach Jesus—sharing only pieces of our lives with Him. We tend to categorize our needs; we decide for ourselves which issues, what questions, which needs Jesus might be inclined to address. How would it change the way you talked with Jesus about what is going on in your life if you realized that He intended to do so much more than you could anticipate?

2. Even those who have walked with Jesus for a long time can end up with questions. We aren't sure why He does the things He does. We aren't clear on what He wants for us. When we have such questions, we can end up allowing the questions to draw us away from Him rather than bringing all our questions to Him. What "reasonings in your heart" are you hesitant to bring to Jesus? What questions seem a bit too troubling to raise? Take some time to move close . . . and ask Him all those questions, raise all those troubling issues. And then listen to what He says to you in response.

3. The paralyzed man's four friends were desperate. They went to extreme lengths to get their friend in front of Jesus. You might not have a physically paralyzed friend in need of Jesus' touch;

you likely won't have to unroof a roof to get a needy friend close to Jesus. But to what lengths will you go—how desperate are you—to have the needs of those you love brought before Jesus? Are you that impressed with Jesus that you see the need to bring your friends to Him? Stop and reflect on those who matter to you; think about the needs in their lives. And begin to pray—fervently, desperately—bringing them before Jesus in prayer in confidence that He will do exceedingly abundantly beyond all that we can think or ask.

FOR GROUP DISCUSSION:

1. What do you think it would have been like for the four friends to unroof the roof in order to let their friends down before Jesus? What would the experience have been like for them? Why would they have gone to such lengths?

2. What did Jesus do for the paralyzed man? List all the things that must have happened to him for him to be able to get up, pick up his bed, and carry the pallet out of the room in front of all those people. What does this reveal to you about Jesus?

3. Do you think the scribes' question was legitimate? Why or why not? What does the way Jesus responds to their question tell you about Him?

CHAPTER SIX

ANYTHING BUT THAT

THE HEALING OF THE MAN WITH THE WITHERED HAND

And He said to the man, "Stretch out your hand." And he stretched it out, and his hand was restored.

—Mark 3:5b

I CAN RECALL THINKING ABOUT how my son's soccer coach was guiding my son through the season. Chris is a good soccer player, but his skill level wasn't quite up to the rest of the guys. He had broken a toe the previous season, and so hadn't played much. He had good ball sense and a desire to play; he just needed some refinement of his skills. But that's hard to tell an eager middle school boy who just wants to play the game.

Chris and I had lots of discussions as the season went on. We talked about his discouragement over not being able to play as much as he would like. We thought out loud about why the coach wasn't letting him play a different position and why he was assigned to the defense. He wasn't getting a chance to score. That is, after all, every budding soccer star's sole desire.

We talked about the coach's experience and his ability to help players improve. I encouraged Chris to stick with it, hoping all along that the coach knew what he was doing and would find the best fit for Chris on the team.

It happened. As the season progressed, the team's standing in the league continued to go up. Chris was playing a good deal, but always defense. But he was good at it; apparently the coach knew that. He had given Chris an assignment that fit him, as well as giving him a role that needed to be filled if the team was going to succeed.

As the season came to a close and Chris' team beat their long-time rivals (something that hadn't happened in years!), he was thrilled. He was appropriately proud that no one in the game had scored from his side of the field when he was in at defense. He had learned how the game could turn on a few good defensive plays and how his skills fit him to play that particular role.

And Chris came to appreciate the coach's wisdom. It was a good season—and a good lesson.

That is something that I need to take to heart when I think of my relationship with Jesus. You see, I'm learning something by watching my son grow. Chris realized he would have to trust his coach's judgment and experience. And he did. And he learned and grew.

And so it is with Jesus and us. We have to learn to trust Him. When we do, we get to grow and learn. And it is just that kind of thinking that is at the heart of another of Jesus' miracles.

IT BEGAN LIKE ANY OTHER WEEKEND

As Jesus' ministry grew, He ran into trouble with some of the Jewish religious leaders. It seemed the way He was approaching life with God was different from the way they approached it. They were having a hard time seeing things from His point of view. So they sought to trip Him up, in the hope of overturning His growing popularity. And one Sabbath morning, their plans didn't turn out like they had hoped.

> And He entered again into a synagogue; and a man was there with a withered hand. And they were watching Him to see if He would heal him on the Sabbath, in order that they might accuse Him.
>
> And He said to the man with the withered hand, "Rise and come forward."
>
> And He said to them, "Is it lawful on the Sabbath to do good, or to do harm, to save a life or to kill?" But they kept silent.
>
> And after looking around at them with anger, grieved at their hardness of heart, He said to the man, "Stretch out your hand." And he stretched it out, and his hand was restored.
>
> And the Pharisees went out immediately and began taking counsel with the Herodians against Him, as to how they might destroy Him.
>
> —Mark 3:1–7

I don't know about you, but when I am not feeling physically my best, I don't really want to be in the spotlight. It's hard enough having to stand up and lead a song, share a thought, offer a prayer, or meet a need when I am feeling physically fit and rested. It's altogether another story when I am not feeling 100 percent. There's just too great a risk of not accomplishing well what needs to be done. When I'm not "all there," the potential for embarrassment goes up and the likelihood that I will perform well goes down.

It seems like most people are that way. We don't like to have attention called to us when we aren't at our best. If it's a bad hair day, you don't want to have to stand up and tell us about yourself. If you've got a migraine, you'd really prefer not to make that big presentation to the company's new client. If your stomach is doing somersaults over something you ate for lunch, then, given the choice, you won't be running the VBS program in your backyard. But, sometimes, we do find ourselves in just such a place—not feeling our best and yet finding the spotlight of attention has somehow settled on us.

I think something like that must have been going through the mind of the man with the withered hand when he showed up to listen to Jesus teach. He, undoubtedly, was at least a little embarrassed about his condition. In those days, it was not uncommon to think of any kind of disfigurement as some kind of notice from God that things weren't right in your life.[61] But having heard Jesus teach (or at least heard of Him), this man braced himself and showed up at the synagogue . . . only to have happen about the worst thing that could.

"Excuse me, Sir. Yes, you with the crippled and deformed hand. Would you come here, please?"

Jesus was speaking to this man. Jesus was calling attention to him. Jesus wanted him to stand up and come front and center. All eyes were going to be on him. And, apparently, he was going to be some sort of object lesson for some of Jesus' critics.

I can't imagine the man feeling much else but apprehension in such a situation. Even knowing Jesus' reputation for healing, to be brought front and center was bound to be a bit flustering. After all, *everyone* in the city had *not* been healed. Jesus healed many, but He didn't heal all, every time.[62] What would happen this time?

There are two things we must notice about Jesus and what He is doing in this situation. First, He is aware that the religious "police" are there and are watching Him in hopes of catching Him doing something[63] they can use to create trouble for Him.[64] It is clear that He is fully aware of that.

This means that when Jesus called this man forward, He intends for what is about to happen to be a point of instruction for others. To put it simply, Jesus is using the man and his situation for a teaching illustration.

Now most of us don't like being used. And, at first glance, that is certainly what it looks like here. Jesus, with His eye on the religious leaders who are watching Him, invites the man forward to teach them a lesson. How would you feel?

IT'S NOT JUST ABOUT . . .

Because I am beginning to get to know Jesus, I think I can comfortably assert that He is not calling this man forward to humiliate him, make a spectacle of him, or simply use him. Jesus is just not that kind of man. But Jesus is going to put His grace and glory on display in the man in a public way—something worth noting.

Although sometimes Jesus did His miracles in a quiet way—even telling people not to say anything about it[65]—at other times He did what He did in clear view of many. This is one of those latter situations.

Sometimes what Jesus does in us and for us may have implications for others. It is not that He is using us, as much as He is bringing us a blessing and simply letting others in on it.

Perhaps that makes you uncomfortable. I can't imagine that this man was not a little uncomfortable with having to stand up and come forward. But remember, the point wasn't to embarrass him or make a spectacle of him. It was, ultimately, for his good and God's glory.

There is a rightful sense that whatever God is doing in all of our lives is really for public display. God is showing His glory in saving us,[66] in making us holy, in reproducing the character of His Son in us. What God is doing in us is not merely for our personal consumption. He intends to receive glory for what He does in and through us. Just like Jesus is going to do with this man.

But let's look a little closer at what Jesus actually asks the man to do.

IT WAS IMPOSSIBLE

After Jesus called the man forward and asked him to stand there in the presence of all, He made one simple request: "Stretch forth your hand."

Do you realize how that would have struck the man?

Here was a man with a withered hand. The hand is disfigured, useless. Apparently it was like an old, lifeless, gnarled tree. Certainly the man could do little, if anything, with the hand. But one of the things he *couldn't* do with it was "stretch it out."

But that is what Jesus asked.

Was Jesus being cruel? He didn't ask the man if he believed He could heal him. He didn't tell the man He was going to heal him. Perhaps the man could have concluded from Jesus' remarks about doing good on the Sabbath that something good was going to happen. The man might have anticipated that possibility.

But Jesus asked him to do what was impossible. The man hadn't stretched out that hand for quite some time. The man couldn't stretch out that hand. But that is what Jesus asked him to do.

I wonder, if I had been that man, what I might have done.

"Jesus, ask me to stretch out the good hand. I'll do that! I'll wave it in the air. Do you want me to show you I love you? I will shout and jump and worship."

"Jesus, as soon as I feel Your power moving through that hand, I'll stretch it out. As soon as I see it good as new, as soon as it looks and feels like the other, I'll stretch it out."

But neither of those responses were what Jesus wanted. He asked the man to stretch out his withered hand. Here's the really amazing and thrilling and life-changing thing: the man did just that!

You see, in giving in to Jesus' command and stretching out that withered hand, it was restored. It was made whole, as good as the other.

In seeing that, I get a fascinating fresh glimpse into this Jesus I am learning to live with.

I NEVER WOULD HAVE THOUGHT . . .

I think it was during a training time at InterVarsity Christian Fellowship headquarters in Madison, Wisconsin, that I got into a conversation with Becky Manley-Pippert (who went on to write a book on evangelism called *Out of the Salt Shaker*). The subject? Jesus. The issue? How He constantly seems to cause crises for people, even His closest followers, even those He is seeking to help. In fact, I think I could reasonably say that Jesus is the most crisis-causing person I have ever met.

Now you may think it improper to think of Jesus in such a way, but it doesn't take long to see how true it is. Jesus causes crises because He calls those He loves out of the difficulty and struggle and trouble they are in, and invites them into something fresh and new. But the fresh and new, being unfamiliar, is sometimes scarier than the old—regardless of how bad the old and familiar might be.

This man, the one with the withered hand, knew what it was like to live as a cripple. He had become accustomed to living with his handicap. He may not have liked it, but at least it was familiar. He knew how to cope. No surprises.

But then he meets Jesus. And Jesus calls him to do the one thing he is sure he cannot do. Jesus throws him into crisis. The man has to risk embarrassment, pain, and distress of body and soul to respond to Jesus' invitation. The only alternative would have been to just ignore Jesus' call, overlook the moment of crisis, and remain crippled.

What would you have done?

I'll let you in on a secret. I'm not sure I would have easily or readily "stretched forth my hand." Why do I say that? Because I can think of countless times Jesus has asked me to stretch out some withered part of my soul, and I have balked.

Perhaps it is the discomfort and disillusionment of some relationship, where you feel you have already put up with more than your share of grief and trouble. And it is there that Jesus asks you to stretch forth your withered love, your crippled forgiveness, your dried-up compassion.

Maybe it is in some area of service where you thought He had been calling you, but where you see little or no fruit. You feel dried out and dried up, frustrated and fruitless. And you hear Him calling you to stretch out your seemingly powerless gifts, your emaciated faith, your nearly nonexistent hope.

I am troubled by what will happen if I reach out, if I stretch out, if I step out in response to His call. This is a crisis moment. The present, with all its troubles, is familiar. What He calls me to is . . . well, it's beyond me! It's impossible. It's risky. It's scary.

But that's what He does.

Jesus may ask challenging things of us. He may request you to do something you wouldn't think of doing in a thousand years. But He will only ask you to do the things that His power will take you through.

That is what we see here, in His dealings with the man with the withered hand. I don't intend to allegorize this healing; the man's withered hand doesn't represent something else. He had a crippled hand. And it was a crippled hand that he stretched out. And it was a crippled hand that Jesus healed.

But the idea extends beyond the reach of the man's hand. The idea that Jesus may well call us beyond what we *know* we can do—only to provide all we need to respond to the call—is something we must see in this account.

A quick glimpse at other encounters that Jesus has with people underscores this idea that Jesus might call us to do what He knows we will not be able to do apart from His help. Jesus calls people to do the impossible. Like calling lame people to walk, telling blind people to see, insisting that a fisherman walk on water, or demanding that dead people arise. But with Jesus' "impossible command" comes the enablement to do that very thing that is perceived to be impossible.

He never commands anything He doesn't intend to have happen—with His help.

Jesus will never lead you somewhere He cannot keep you. He will never put you in a situation He will not bring you through. He will not have you risk in a way that He has not already undertaken to make sure there really is no risk. He will only ask of us—of you, of me—what His grace and power and love and goodness will ensure can and will happen.

So Jesus was not thinking of embarrassing the man, but of healing the man. He was not intending to put him at risk, but to make him whole. He was not using the man, but working through the man for His glory. And in this man, Jesus' power was seen in a fresh and glorious way.

He is not thinking of embarrassing you, either, but of bringing you to greater health. He is not intending to put you at risk, but to bring you to greater wholeness. He does not use you, but He does work through you for His glory. And when we give in to His call, His power can be seen in us in a fresh and glorious way. Even in your life and my life.

And that is just like Jesus.

So, as you feel Jesus' tug on your heart or hear His call to step out in a way that initially might make you feel uncomfortable, remember—He is intending to use your life as a prism through which the magnificent rainbow of His grace and goodness and glory is going to be seen. So take a deep breath, get your eyes on Him, and step on out. Stretch out your hand—whatever part of you He calls for—regardless of how withered you may feel. There is health and wholeness coming.

REFLECTING ON THIS TRUTH

FOR PERSONAL REFLECTION

1. Many times we hesitate to do even the plain things of Scripture because we feel incapacitated. I have met many Christians who will say, "I just can't forgive" (although we are told to forgive . . . always). Or "So-and-so is impossible to love" (even though we are told to love other people like Jesus loves). Or "I'm just not patient" (in spite of the invitation to let the Spirit provide us all the patience we will require). Are there any plain things of Scripture that you are avoiding because you feel that it's just not in you to carry out? Why not confess to Him that it isn't in you,

but then ask Him to make His power known through you as you take Him at His word and simply do what He has asked of you.

2. There may be times in your life when you think Jesus is asking of you something you just know you won't be able to do. But can you see, in the account of this miracle, the truth that He will only ask of you what He intends to help you with? That He will only ask of you what He plans on working through in your life for your good and His glory? If you have been holding back from following through on something He has asked of you, tell Him you are ready. Tell Him that you trust Him. Tell Him that at His bidding, you will do whatever He asks of you. And then get ready to see what He will do!

FOR GROUP DISCUSSION

1. If you had been the man with the withered hand, would you have come front and center at Jesus' request? Would you have willingly stretched forth your deformed arm? Why or why not?

2. If there are going to be times when Jesus would like to put His goodness and glory and power on display in and through our weaknesses, what will that mean for how we share with one another about what He is doing in our lives?

3. What do you see about Jesus that will make it easier for you to trust Him when he calls you to trust Him about things in your life that are uncomfortable to face?

CHAPTER SEVEN

WHAT WOULD YOU HAVE DONE?

STILLING THE STORM

And Jesus got up and rebuked the wind and said to the sea, "Hush, be still." And the wind died down and it became perfectly calm.

—Mark 4:39

"MONDAY MORNING QUARTERBACKING." THAT'S WHAT it's called when armchair athletes get together the day after the big game and explain how things should have been done so their favorite team would have won, rather than lost. These analysts-from-a-distance, drawing on a couple of years of high school or college ball, feel they have what it takes to have pulled the game out.

We all do it. When *you* are not the one facing the pressure, when *you* are not in the thick of it, when *you* are watching from a distance, it's easy to explain what *someone else* should have done in order to turn defeat into victory, embarrassment into a social coup, or a broken relationship into an enduring friendship. Although we don't all quarterback the team from the water cooler, we all tend to think that if we had been part of the latest troubling turn of events, it would have turned out completely different.

It's not wrong to think that we might have approached a particularly bad situation differently from someone we know. It is good we can see options that they may have overlooked. But hindsight does tend to be much better than foresight. Looking back on what could have been different seems to be much easier than looking ahead to see what should be.

One of the places where this advisor-from-afar problem can lead us astray is when we open the Bible. Reading the Gospel accounts of what those early followers of Jesus did can leave us thinking, "I would never have done that!" At least we think that way when we watch them mess up, something they do fairly frequently.

But when we see ourselves in such a different light than those Jesus handpicked to learn from Him, we hinder our ability to learn the lessons they learned. We act as if we've already arrived, and short-circuit the possibility that there is something in their experience we can learn from.

The writers of the Gospels recorded the lives of real people, people just like you and me. If we read the accounts of the words and works of Jesus with a willingness to find ourselves in the action (rather than offering color commentary from the sidelines) we might gain more insight about ourselves and about our Friend and Savior, Jesus.

So, let's look at a short, familiar miracle account—one involving the disciples. And rather than trying to evaluate the situation from a distance, let's enter in to see what it would have been like to be there, with Jesus.

IT WAS A DARK AND STORMY NIGHT

If you attentively read the Gospels, it seems that Jesus has the disciples on a slightly different learning track than the multitude who were following Him. He teaches the multitude, but He explains things to His closest twelve.[67] He ministers broadly and touches many lives, but then He takes these dozen on a separate journey for some private instruction. Because of the Gospels, we are privy not only to what Jesus shared with the masses, but we get to sit in the school of the disciples and learn with them.

Jesus had been teaching the multitude just before the episode we will be reading. He had been teaching in parables, illustrating what the Kingdom is like. And then He has been explaining things in plainer language to the Twelve. (I wonder if that could be not so much because they were the "best of the best," but because they were the "remedial class" and needed some extra attention. All kidding aside, don't think of the Twelve as some kind of rare breed; they were no different than the others. Jesus simply needed a core group to work with, and they were the ones He chose.[68]) After the teaching time, the lesson has not quite come to an end. We pick up what happens next in Mark.

> And on that day, when evening had come, He said to them, "Let us go over to the other side." And leaving the multitude, they took Him along with them, just as He was, in the boat; and other boats were with Him.

> And there arose a fierce gale of wind, and the waves were breaking over the boat so much that the boat was already filling up. And He Himself was in the stern, asleep on the cushion; and they awoke Him and said to Him, "Teacher, do you not care that we are perishing?"
>
> And being aroused, He rebuked the wind and said to the sea, "Hush, be still." And the wind died down and it became perfectly calm. And He said to them, "Why are you so timid? How is it that you have no faith?"
>
> And they became much afraid and said to one another, "Who then is this, that even the wind and sea obey Him?"
>
> —Mark 4:35–41

There is only one way to understand this episode. We have to climb into the boat with the Twelve. We have to journey with them out on to the sea. We have to join them that evening.[69] Only then will we begin to grasp what happened.

As you may recall, at least four of these men were professional fisherman—Simon Peter and his brother Andrew, as well as the brothers James and John.[70] They had made their living traveling the waters of the Sea of Galilee. Seeing as they often fished at night, they undoubtedly had made their share of night crossings.[71] No doubt they had also experienced their fair share of storms while at sea at night.[72]

Twelve men. Accustomed to hard life (well, with the possible exception of Levi, the tax man!) and traveling across this lake late at night. And a storm came up. Let's join them in boat.

GOING ALONG FOR THE RIDE

How serious a storm was it? Mark tells us it was a fierce gale. This is a frightening storm. We are in the boat, and the waves are beginning to break over the boat. We are not merely being tossed by the waves. The waves are cresting so huge that they come crashing down into the boat. As seaworthy as this fishing vessel is, it is beginning to take on water.

We bale and steer and manage as best as we can for a while. Things are not getting better, though; they are getting worse. This is no parable, no moral tale. This really is happening as we ride in the boat across the sea.

It's a pitch-dark night. The lightning is flashing and thunder crashing. You can feel the water in the boat up to your knees. With each swell, more water spills over and into the boat, soaking you and drawing the boat deeper into the water. Sturdy men all, we begin to fear for our lives. We are on the brink of sinking, of losing our lives.

What do you do? There you are, soaked to the skin, freezing in the gale, up to your knees in water with more coming in all the time. You began to see the boat list to one side—a sure sign it's about to go under. What do you do?

I am fairly sure about what I would have done.

These men had walked with Jesus for some time now. They had seen Him do some amazing things. Although they may not yet know fully who He is, they have begun to see that God is with Him in a powerful and unique way. A quick glance tells them He is still sleeping; He must be exhausted to sleep through this.

I know what I would have done.

I don't know if these men knew exactly what Jesus might do. Seeing that they feared for their lives, they must have thought He might be able to do something. Obviously, they would not have woken Him up if they thought He would be useless! (At least He could help them bail.)

I would have done just what they did. I would have woken Jesus with the expectation that He would do something about the dire situation we were in. He must be able to do something to help. We must wake Him! This situation is desperate! Isn't that what you would have done?

JUST IN THE NICK OF TIME

So Jesus is roused. It takes Him but a moment to take in the situation. He, too, is soaked to the skin. He feels the waves and the spray. But He is not panicked. He rises and speaks, loud enough to be heard over the storm. Simple words. Powerful words.

"Hush!" (Literally, He tells the wind and the storm to "be muzzled!") "Be still."

And it becomes perfectly calm. Stunning! Amazing!

There we sit, almost giddy. Moments ago, we were sure that this storm would be the end of us. Now we are sure we did the right thing in waking Jesus because at His word everything is calm. The wind has died down to a whisper. The waves have stopped their hammering of the boat. The rocking has abated. The splashing is gone. What relief! What joy! We are safe. It was right to wake Him. He was a great help.

And then Jesus turns to us—to those in the boat—and says: "How is it that you have no faith?"

Do you hear what He is saying? To those who called on Him when they needed Him the most, to those who cried out to Him because they hoped and believed and knew He could do something, to those who staked their lives on His help. It is to *them* He raised this question.

How can Jesus rightly accuse these men (and us with them) of not having faith? What else could we have done? What else should we have done? We went to Him because we thought, because we knew, He could do something. Isn't that the essence of faith?

In order to understand what has happened, we need to be careful readers. It is not that there is something secret hidden in the passage, but in order to answer the question as to why Jesus questioned the disciples this way we need to be attentive to what occurred.

WHAT THEIR OUTSIDE TELLS US ABOUT THEIR INSIDES

Besides their waking Jesus up, we get an indication of what is going on in the heart of the disciples by what comes out of their mouths. What they say is a reflection of the condition of their faith.

They must have thought Jesus could do something to help them; they had faith in Him in that sense. They wouldn't have woken Him only to say their last goodbyes. It is in their waking Him that we catch a glimpse of what is in their hearts.

Notice what they said: "Do you not care that we are perishing?"

Apparently the disciples didn't doubt Jesus could do something. What was lacking was a certainty, in the midst of the storm, that Jesus cared for them. Certainty that Jesus does genuinely care for me is at the heart of true faith in a Biblical sense.

(The devils, we are told, "believe" but they tremble. Why? Because they acknowledge the great power of God but realize it is not "for" them![73])

It is here that I identify with the disciples.

In the day-to-day, I don't spend much time thinking about Jesus' love for me. I live with something of the sense of "that's a given." Then some trouble strikes, some difficulty presents itself. If you were to ask me at such times, "*Can* Jesus do something about this?" I will tell you, "Of course!" But I still struggle.

I wonder: Is Jesus aware? Has He noticed that things aren't going so well for me? Is He touched with the trouble that touches me? Does He really *care*? If I am not convinced of His care, I am left wondering whether He will act. And that is what the disciples questioned.

They had been with Him long enough to know. They had shared meals and adventures and starry nights out under the Palestinian night sky with Him. They knew, on some level, that Jesus cared. But when the waves came and the trouble mounted, what percolated to the top of their hearts was this haunting thought: "I wonder if He really does care?"

That is the cry they raise in waking Him. That is the confession that prompts His mild rebuke.

WHEN THAT CRY COMES OUT OF MY HEART

It is easy for me to sing the words, "Jesus loves me, this I know." I can make a persuasive case for Jesus' love for you. But I wonder, at times, about Jesus' disposition toward me. Is He merely putting up with me? Does He just tolerate me? Does He really care?

That issue is of greatest concern when facing a challenge. We don't often hold an internal debate about whether the Creator and Sustainer of All has sufficient *resources* to rescue us from the waves that threaten to roll over us. Our only question is whether He *cares enough* to *do* something.

No armchair analysts here. If we join the disciples in the boat, we find ourselves doing just what they would have done. And we might well have received the same gentle nudge.

"How is it that you have no faith? Don't you realize that I do care? I will not abandon you!"

A PREVIEW OF COMING ATTRACTIONS

There is one other component to Jesus' rebuke. He questioned the faith of the disciples beyond the question of His care for them—but why?

Before getting into the boat that night to make the trip across the sea, Jesus had been teaching them. The subject of the lesson? "Taking care" what you listen to (Mark 4:24).

Jesus had told them that He was sowing "the word." He explained that the word He was sowing—what He was saying—was essential to living in the Kingdom. He elaborated by saying that the Kingdom works in accordance with the words Jesus sows. Even if someone doesn't know how the Kingdom life will work out, Jesus' words will bring growth.[74]

When Jesus and His friends get into the boat, He tells them, "Let us go over to the other side." Listen again: "Let us go over to the other side."

Those were not idle words. Jesus always says what He means and means what He says. He didn't say to them, "Let's try and cross." He didn't say, "It looks pretty frightening, I wonder if we'll make it." He did say, "We're going all the way across."

One of the things you will see as you walk with the disciples through their three years with Jesus is that He often teaches them something and then gives them, almost immediately, an opportunity to "put it into practice." Not in a conniving way but in an intentional way, He sets them up to own the truth they have been hearing.

Is it possible that part of what Jesus wants is for them to take Him at His word? After all, He did tell them they were going to go all the way across. Not, "Let's all drown in the middle of the lake."

When you first read the passage (and also, no doubt, if you were there living through the passage), what Jesus had said about going across may not have seemed like either a promise or a command. It likely seemed just . . . well, just a comment. You know, like, "Let's go."

But living with Jesus and growing to trust Him means growing to take Him at His word, at all times. It means listening very carefully to what He says, because He doesn't "sow" idle words.

Again, right here, I identify with the disciples. In the midst of trouble, I can find myself fretting, panicked, and anxious. I might have a certain kind of general confidence in Jesus' ability and power. What I am often unsure of, though, is what Jesus has said about the situation I am facing.

I think, at times, I am guilty of selective listening. I don't give full attention to all Jesus says to me—whether in the words I find in the Scripture or the words He speaks to my heart. A call to repent from some habit as He is drawing me into a deeper experience of holiness that I don't take seriously. An invitation to participate more fully in the life of the community of faith that to better experience His life that I dismiss as generic. I end up disappointed with how things are and cry out to Him, all the while ignoring some of what He has been saying to me. I may not have paid much attention to His specific word to me.

It might be that Jesus' chastening of the Twelve was also rooted in this. After all, He had already told them something they could have hung on to. They were going to make it. They weren't going to drown—even if they didn't know how they were going to make it. But that was what He had said. They could have been certain they would make it all the way across.

WHEN THE GOING GETS TOUGH

So, what could the disciples have done differently? Was it wrong to wake Jesus? Should they have tried to figure out, on their own, what to do?

I think waking Jesus was right. Whenever we face difficulties, we can call on Him. In fact, we *should* call on Him. He is, after all, our very present help in time of need.[75] It makes sense. Call on Him.

But when you do, remember what happened in the boat. Remember how the disciples woke Him.

They questioned whether He really cared.

Do you do that when you call on Him? Do you raise a doubt about His tender compassion and kindness toward you? Do you debate within your heart about whether He really cares enough to act?

Don't! Jesus isn't like that. He will not leave you.[76] He will not let His friends go through such things alone. He wants to be of help.[77] So call on Him. Don't hesitate to do so. Just don't call on Him with that questioning tone in your voice. Don't debate whether He really does care for you.

They didn't take Him fully at His word.

Do you do that when you call on Him? Have you not been listening? Are you unsure of what He has said to you? Do you debate whether He will actually fulfill what He said about seeing you through, sustaining you throughout, filling you thoroughly? Do you hold an internal discussion about whether He really meant what He said?

Don't! Jesus isn't like that. He will be true to His word. If He said He will never leave you or forsake you, He will be there. If He said that in every situation He will give you peace, He will give it abundantly. If He said that you will be led by His grace through whatever comes so that you will look more like Him, that is what you should expect will happen.

Know that He loves you. He really cares. Know that He will be true to His word. He will do all He says.

And let the waves come and the winds blow. We are going to the other side.

REFLECTING ON THIS TRUTH

FOR PERSONAL REFLECTION

1. Do you feel that there are some storms ahead in your life? Maybe you are already feeling the waves break across your life. And you want to call out to Jesus for help. That's okay. Don't hold back. But before you ask Him to act on your behalf, reflect on Psalm 63—it is one of David's meditations on the Lord's unfailing love for us.

2. In a time of need, you may need to do a little homework. That is, if you are facing a particular kind of trouble—for example, trouble in relationships—you might have to pull out your Bible and find some passages where the Lord tells you what He intends to do in such situations. It's hard to trust Him if you don't know what He said He would do. A concordance would be of help (or a good friend with a familiarity with the Bible!). But don't be reluctant to look through His Word to find out what He has said about your particular trouble. He's true to His Word. Look for what He has said He'll do. And then, ask Him for that. He'll come through.

FOR GROUP DISCUSSION

1. One of the issues that leads Jesus to ask about the disciples' lack of faith is their question of His care. How can we speak to one another to help overcome that common question of Jesus' care for us?

2. What Jesus says really does matter. What keeps us from being attentive to His words to us? Why do we find ourselves ignoring the simple things He tells us?

3. In facing a recent (or current) challenge, which of these issues do you find most causes you to stumble—questioning His care, or failing to recall His words to you? How can you address this stumbling block in your own life?

CHAPTER EIGHT

WHAT DID HE SAY?

THE RESTORATION OF THE DEAF AND DUMB MAN

And they were utterly astonished, saying, "He has done all things well; He makes even the deaf to hear, and the dumb to speak."

—Mark 7:37

IT HAS TO BE ONE of those great movie moments. The opening few minutes of "The Sound of Music."[78] Music plays softly in the background. We are flying over the Alps. We soar around majestic, snow-capped mountains. The camera takes us weaving through rich, green valleys. We catch the glimpse of villages in the distance.

Then the camera focuses on a figure in the distance. The music becomes the background for her vocals. As the camera closes in, we see Maria—singing, dancing, and thoroughly enjoying "her" mountains.

The sweeping panorama is not wasted time. It is not just a place to run the credits. Those moments set the stage for all that follows. Although we don't get many details as we soar through the mountains, we do get a feel for what will follow. The grand sweep of things, the lay of the land so to speak, is laid out for us in those opening grand moments.

But once the camera zooms in on Maria, we need to be attentive to her. The director has been intentional. He has designed a certain part of his message to be told only in the broad-brush strokes of the flight through the Alps. But he also intends for us to now be attentive to the details of what is happening, as the camera focuses closely on Maria herself.

WITH BROAD STROKES

Under the inspiration of the Spirit, the authors of the Gospels employ a similar approach. In recording for us the good news about Jesus, there are times they whisk us through days or weeks of ministry in a few sentences. We are given only a "fly over" sort of report of all that Jesus was saying and doing. In a few short statements, they give us a glimpse—the glimpse they want us to have—of the broad setting for the life and ministry of Jesus.

Then, when they want us to be attentive, they bring the focus in close onto Jesus. They draw us right into the middle of what He is doing. There, in that moment, we need to be attentive. This is not to be glossed over. We need to look closely.

This rhythm of sweeping vistas and intriguing close-ups is evident when you look at the miracles of Jesus. At times, the Gospel writers will say things like this:

> And when He came out, He saw a great multitude, and felt compassion for them, and healed their sick.
>
> —Matthew 14:14

> And the whole city was gathered at the door. And He healed many who were ill with various diseases, and cast out many demons.
>
> —Mark 1:34

> And He descended with them, and stood on a level place; and there was a great multitude of His disciples, and a great throng of people from all Judea and Jerusalem and the coastal region of Tyre and Sidon, who had come to hear Him, and to be healed of their diseases; and those who were troubled by unclean spirits were being cured. And all the multitude were trying to touch Him, for power was coming from Him and healing them all.
>
> —Luke 6:17–19

The Gospel authors are giving us the big picture; they are providing the fly-over view. In doing this, they solidify the truth that Jesus was, in fact, doing miracles and healing people and working wonderful signs in a great way. If all they wanted was for us to know that Jesus did such things, they might have left it at that. We would have only the grand vistas.

But as the Spirit directed them in their writing, they often focus closely on what Jesus did. When they do that, we need to be aware that they are not simply telling us "Jesus healed a person" or "Jesus did a miracle." The details demand our attention.

When they wanted us to have a summary, they gave us one. But when the camera pulls in close, they are telling us something more.

HE WASN'T PLAYING GAMES

What does Jesus *have* to do to heal someone? A simple answer is evident in the Gospel accounts. All Jesus must do to heal someone is to say it, to will it. The Gospels are filled with accounts of Jesus healing people. Typically, Jesus heals by a touch or even by His word alone.[79] But that is not all we find in the Gospels. Sometimes we find something quite atypical.

Let's take a look at one of the up-close accounts from the Gospel of Mark. Because it is a close up, we will need to pay attention to the details.

> And again He went out from the region of Tyre, and came through Sidon to the Sea of Galilee, within the region of Decapolis. And they brought to Him one who was deaf and spoke with difficulty, and they entreated Him to lay His hand upon him.
>
> And He took him aside from the multitude by himself, and put His fingers into his ears, and after spitting, He touched his tongue; and looking up to heaven with a deep sigh, He said to him, Ephphatha!" that is, "Be opened!"
>
> And his ears were opened, and the impediment of his tongue was removed, and he began speaking plainly.

> And He gave them orders not to tell anyone; but the more He ordered them, the more widely they continued to proclaim it. And they were utterly astonished, saying, "He has done all things well; He makes even the deaf to hear, and the dumb to speak."
>
> —Mark 7:31–37

What is so striking about this particular miracle account is how Jesus interacts with this man. For, after all, He did not have to go through all these motions in order to bring the man to full health. He is not playing games with the man. But Jesus didn't *have* to do these things in order to heal the man, so the natural question is, why does Jesus do this?

With R. C. Trench, we could affirm that Jesus did this because, in His wisdom, He deemed it best.

> That there must lie a deep meaning in all the variations which mark the different healings of different sick and afflicted, a wisdom of God ordering all the circumstances of each particular cure . . . why one was healed in the crowd, and another led out of the city before the work of restoration was commenced; why for one a word effected a cure, for another a touch, while a third was sent to wash in the pool of Siloam ere 'he came seeing' . . . . Our ignorance may prevent us from at once and in every case discerning 'the manifold wisdom' which ordered each work of his, but we are not less sure that this wisdom ordered them all.[80]

It might be true that we are left in ignorance about why Jesus did what he did. But I wonder what we might find if we probed a little deeper.

Mark has laid out certain details for us. Jesus did what He did with a purpose. Reading attentively might disclose things in the text that can reveal to us something about why Jesus did what He did. The way forward? Put yourself in the situation and think through what is really happening. Don't just read the words on the page; enter into the account and picture what Mark is telling you.

DO AS I DO

Jesus has disembarked in the region of the Decapolis; this is a predominantly Gentile region. Mark's only other mention of Jesus being here is in Mark 5 where Jesus delivered a demoniac living in the tombs. Jesus had then sent that man to tell everyone what He had done for him. Mark tells us the formerly demonized man "went off and began to proclaim in Decapolis what great things Jesus had done for him; and everyone marveled" (Mark 5:10).

So because of this former demoniac's testimony, when it is learned that Jesus is back in the vicinity, a crowd gathers. It is in the midst of the great commotion that some people work their way through the crowd bringing another fellow. They led him along; that is not surprising because of the man's debilities. The camera pulls in close as Jesus comes face to face with this particular man.

Jesus could have merely spoken a word or reached out a hand and this deaf and dumb man would have been restored. But that is not what He does.

He takes the man off to the side away from the crowd.

He thrusts[81] His fingers in the man's ears.

He spits.

He touches the man's tongue with His finger.[82]

He looks up to heaven.

He sighs.

And then He says, "Be opened," and the man is healed.

Of all that Jesus did, what was necessary for the man to be healed? Jesus only had to say the word. He could have looked at the man, said "Be open," and the man would have been made well. What's with all the other stuff, then?

Walk in this man's place—the man about to be healed—for a moment. Well-intentioned friends come to your home and begin dragging you somewhere. They try as best they can to explain to you what is going on. Some of the gestures you can make out, but you just can't tell what excites them so much. You try, but you can't explain to them that you don't want to go out in public.[83] There are enough of them that, in their good intentions, you have no choice but to go along.

You ultimately come to a crowd. You don't like crowds. It's hard to make your way, because you can't shout or ask people to get out of your way, and you can't hear when someone needs you to move. Crowds are unnerving and uncomfortable. But these friends of yours push through the crowd, trailing you with them.

Then they break into a small clearing in the crowd. You are standing face to face with a man you have never met before. Looking at you, He gently takes you by the hand and leads you away from the commotion of the crowd. You follow.

Can you begin to see what is about to happen? Jesus takes this man aside. He isn't doing miracles to put on a show. If He were, He would have healed him right there, in the midst of the crowd. But Jesus isn't like that. He takes the man aside. And then, away from the commotion and chaos of the crowd, Jesus and this man share an incredible moment.

Think about it from the deaf-and-dumb man's perspective. Clearly, Jesus is focusing on him. So think of this account from his point of view.

As Jesus stands before him, He gently but energetically puts His fingers in the man's ears. What would the man be thinking? He must be thinking something like . . .

Well, this man seems to be saying something about my ears. Does he know I am deaf? Of course he can tell; and my friends may have told him. He seems interested in my ears. Could it be . . . is that the reason for all this commotion . . . could it be he can do something about my hearing?

And then Jesus spits. The deaf and dumb man has to think some more.

This man is communicating with me! He is indicating that He's going to do something about my ears. And, what? He's spitting. Does he want me to spit? Is something going to come out of his mouth? But wait . . .

And then Jesus touches the man's tongue. And the man begins to understand . . .

My tongue. He must know I can't speak either . . . that nothing comes out . . . ; but wait! That's it. Something is going to come out of the mouth, but not his mouth, my mouth. Can it be that this man is trying to fix my problems?

And then Jesus looks up to heaven. This sign the man well knows.

Often I have looked up to the heavens, asking God to deliver me from this affliction. And now this man does the same. He must be praying; he must be calling on heaven.

And then Jesus sighs. And the man sees this, too.

What? Why is He sighing? In sadness? Maybe his prayer wasn't heard. Or maybe . . . maybe he is somehow involved in this healing. Maybe he feels something as he prays. Maybe . . .

And then it happens. The man hears the words that end his affliction. "Be opened!"

NOW WE'RE TALKING!

Jesus is not just doing some weird mumbo-jumbo stuff. He is communicating with this man. He is speaking to the man in a way he can understand. But in just a few moments, the man will have full hearing and will be able to speak.[84] So why go through all of this?

Two thoughts stir in my mind. The first is more theological, the other more personal.

In the Gospels, it is clear that Jesus often (although not always) responds to people on the basis of their faith.[85] He reaches into their lives as they look expectantly to Him, as they trust Him to act on their behalf.

Perhaps part of why Jesus communicates with this man in this fashion is to give him the opportunity to trust Him. We don't know how long their exchange took, but in the process the man could have come to anticipate that Jesus was going to do something. The man's faith in Jesus could have blossomed.[86] After all, Jesus is not only concerned about the physical need this man has; He wants to minister to the whole person.[87] The man's soul is as important as his body.

However, Mark has not given us any indication of the state of this man's faith. He may have believed, but we can't say for certain. In fact, in the Gospels, there are examples of Jesus ministering to people who apparently didn't give any evidence of having faith.[88] So, although it could be that the man's faith is being stirred, it is hard to insist that this passage makes that clear.

But there is something else here. I assume that Jesus always does what the Father wants Him to do.[89] Thus, this sign language communication is a necessary part of the interaction. Although not essential to the healing itself, Jesus does this because He must. Not because there is some kind of external list of "things to do when healing a deaf and dumb man," but because of who He is and how He does life. Something about Jesus results in His interacting this way with this man.

NOT AN ASSEMBLY LINE

The deaf and dumb man's friends brought him to Jesus, wanting Jesus to heal him. Why does Mark tell us the details about what happened here? Why bring the camera in close on this episode?

I think Mark wants us to catch a glimpse of Jesus just being Himself. The Spirit is highlighting something important for us.

Do you see what Jesus was doing? He is being personal with the man.

I often hear from people that their physicians treat them as objects. Going in for a surgical procedure, you may be referred to as "the spleen in room 232" or the "blockage we treated yesterday." But Jesus doesn't deal with this man as a healing project. He responds to this man as an individual. He communicates to him, in his language.

In my world, it is easy to think that sometimes all I am is a number. My bank knows me as 0100021002093182. The government has a number they use to identify me. My medical insurance tags me with a string of numbers and processes the claims about my treatment in mathematical ways. Even the telephone solicitor, who calls with such a cheery voice, doesn't really know me; to her I'm just the next number to be called.

In the midst of our complex lives, we can feel as if we are lost in the sea of numbers—that I am really just a "thing" in the midst of a sea of other things needing some attention. But that is not how Jesus sees us.

When Jesus approaches you to touch your life and lift you up and address your needs, He approaches you as an *individual.* He adapts His communication to where you are. He speaks your *language.* He deals with you as a person, a whole person. You are not a "depression in Atlanta" or a "gambler in New Jersey" or a "preacher from Wales" or a "harried mother in Chicago." He knows all about you, He knows your "business" better than you do (as we saw in chapter two), and He intends to interact with you as a person.

This, in fact, is a significant part of what the Incarnation is all about. Jesus became like us, and walked the earth, so that He could interact personally with people as individuals. Although He is no longer physically present, He is no less personal.

Are you any less willing to be personal with your friends when you communicate by phone? By mail? Of course not. No matter how you communicate with those who are dear to you, you do so in as personal a way as you can. And Jesus does the same. Although He isn't physically present in the same way as He was when He walked the streets of Palestine, He is altogether just as personal in His dealings with you.

I AM NOT . . .

There is a powerful scene in the movie *The Elephant Man*.[90] The film is based on the true story of John Merrick, a hideously deformed man who lived in England around the turn of the century, and the gracious Doctor Treeves, who sought to give him as normal, and as human, a life as possible. When John would go out in public, he would have to cover his face entirely, his visage being so terrible that women would faint at the sight of him and children would shriek. John was apparently quite intelligent (and he may even have known the Lord).

As the story unfolds, due to an unfortunate turn of events, John is taken from the care of the man who has treated him so kindly and taken to Europe to be exhibited in a freak show. He escapes, and attempts to return to the only place he had found comfort and normalcy.

Making his way through the streets of London, he accidentally knocks over a little girl, having great difficulty making his way under his hooded mask while nursing the profound limp that characterizes his walk. The crowd milling about, noticing what has happened, begin to shout at him. A chase ensues.

Because the people are put off by John's appearance—even under the hood he wears—the few who initially give chase grow to become a crowd. They pursue John down the alleys, shouting at him. He is finally cornered in a dead end. People are shouting at him, poking at him, wanting him to reveal himself; they want to "deal with" him.

And in that moment John cries out, in a garbled but nonetheless understandable way: "I'm not an animal. I'm a human being!" John is desperate for them to treat him as a person!

I have felt that cry rise in my own heart. In the midst of the struggles every Christian faces, when they are left alone in the dark with the weights of life and a soul that feels it will be crushed under the struggle, I have cried out: "I am not just a pawn in this game of life! I am not just a worker or a husband or a choir member. I am a human being! I am an individual!"

It is right then that Jesus says, "I know. I know you. And it is always My intention to treat you as just that, the unique individual you are." And He begins to speak my language, communicating to me in the ways I uniquely need, so that His grace might flow into and over and through my life, bringing the kind of marvelous transformation that His grace alone can bring.

He knows your language as well. He knows how best to communicate with you. He knows what it will take to open your heart to His grace. He knows the words to say, the things to do; He knows how to treat you as an individual. There is nothing generic about the way Jesus loves you. If you will let Him take you aside from the crowd of life, you will find Him wholly attentive, wholly personal, wholly gracious.

REFLECTING ON THIS TRUTH

FOR PERSONAL REFLECTION:

1. Perhaps your heart and mind have never been captured by the idea that Jesus both knows you intimately and personally and desires a relationship with you that is marked by "personal-ness," but such is the case. Even David had a sense of this personal dimension of relationship with God: it is reflected in his prayer in Psalm 139. Take some time and talk to God about what David wrote in Psalm 139:13–18.

2. It is easy, when our times of prayer are squeezed in between the busyness of life, to never really realize that Jesus wants to speak to us in a way we could really understand. We bring Him our grocery list of requests and, having recited them, we offer a quick word of thanks and we're off. It is hard to experience His personalness when you are attempting to hold a conversation with Him while doing the laundry, driving to work, or playing with the kids. It's not that it is wrong to pray and talk with Him during such times; you can and should "pray without ceasing." But to experience the depth of His personal touch in your life, it may well take at least a few minutes where you are fully attentive to Him. Take time today to listen for Him; don't just talk. You might be surprised at how intimately He speaks to you.

FOR GROUP DISCUSSION:

1. What might change in the way you participated in a worship service if you understood Jesus' desire to treat you personally? What might change in the way you participated in a small group gathering?

2. Jesus' personal approach helps us see that He intends to speak to each of us in ways we can understand. How could coming to understand this change the way you pray? The way you read Scripture?

3. As you explore this miracle account, it will become evident that everyone in your group does not process and think about it exactly the same. How does Jesus' example guide you in thinking about your interaction with others in the group and with their different ways of viewing life?

CHAPTER NINE

IN OVER YOUR HEAD

WALKING ON THE WATER

And Jesus said, "Come!" And Peter got out of the boat, and walked on the water and came toward Jesus.

—Matthew 14:29

SOME PEOPLE WHO HAVE NO business singing don't seem to realize they can't carry a tune. I'm not being cruel, simply honest: some people don't seem to be able to reasonably assess their own abilities.

A singing contestant is quickly evicted when—contrary to what he thought—it turns out he really can't tell one note from another. The speaker drones on and on boring her audience because—contrary to what she thought—she can't hold anyone's attention for long. That weekend warrior hogs the ball only to be shut down every time because—contrary to what he thought—he doesn't have good ball sense.

Most of us have blind spots. We may not see them in ourselves, even though we can point them out in others. Even writing this—about others' blind spots—causes me to wonder what flaws I am overlooking in my own life.

This tendency plays into our reading about the lives of the disciples. In the course of a Bible study, while reading about an embarrassing moment for the friends of Jesus, someone will comment, "I would never have done such a thing." We are ready to point out the weaknesses of the Twelve. Yet I wonder whether, in pointing out their weaknesses, we overlook our own.

We are quick to see ourselves in the best light and others in the worst. That doesn't change much when we come to the disciples. Too often we think we've got it all together and they didn't. But perhaps we aren't reading carefully enough.

Let's look at a miracle where, at first reading, it may seem one of the disciples messed up. But only at first reading.

AFTER YOU!

We are not talking about an obscure incident, but one of the more notable miracles Jesus did. The risk in reading an account so well known is that we tend to assume we know everything that was going on. So, prepare yourself. Don't read the first few words and say, "Oh, yes, I know what happens." Read attentively; read carefully.

It was after Jesus had taught and fed a multitude . . .

> Jesus made the disciples get into the boat, and go ahead of Him to the other side, while He sent the multitudes away. And after He had sent the multitudes away, He

went up to the mountain by Himself to pray; and when it was evening, He was there alone.

But the boat was already many stadia away from the land, battered by the waves; for the wind was contrary. And in the fourth watch of the night He came to them, walking upon the sea. And when the disciples saw Him walking on the sea, they were frightened, saying, "It is a ghost!" And they cried out for fear.

But immediately Jesus spoke to them, saying, "Take courage, it is I; do not be afraid."

And Peter answered Him and said, "Lord, if it is You, command me to come to You on the water."

And He said, "Come!" And Peter got out of the boat, and walked on the water and came toward Jesus. But seeing the wind, he became afraid, and beginning to sink, he cried out saying, "Lord, save me!"

And immediately Jesus stretched out His hand and took hold of him and said to him, "O you of little faith, why did you doubt?"

And when they got into the boat, the wind stopped. And those who were in the boat worshipped Him, saying, "You are certainly God's Son!"

—Matthew 14:22–33

Peter seems to get himself into a lot of trouble. And this wouldn't be the only time.

A short time earlier Peter had confessed that he believed Jesus was the Son of God (Matthew 16:16).[91] Yet moments later Peter turned around and tried to tell Jesus what He needed to do (Matthew 16:22–23).[92] You may recall that it was Peter who denied knowing Jesus when Jesus was arrested and was brought before the ruling council in Jerusalem (Matthew 26:70–74). All too often, Peter doesn't respond in the best possible way. Maybe that is the case here.

Knowing the kind of guy he is, it might be easy to conclude that Peter is just doing something wrong . . . again. He must not be firing on all cylinders. And here, he even gets rebuked by Jesus. Or so it seems.

Let's get in the boat with Peter and the others. Let's brave the storm. Let's watch Jesus as He comes walking on the water. And let's try and think about what we might have done.

IT'S BEEN A LONG . . . AND TROUBLING . . . NIGHT.

The disciples are somewhere in the middle of the lake, although they should have been across by now. Imagine yourself in that mix.

Accustomed to travel across this relatively small body of water, we would have expected to have reached landfall. We started out at dusk; it is now between three and six in the morning.[93]

We are cold, tired, wet, and frustrated. If only the storm would subside for a while, we could get to land. Every eye is straining to see some indication of safe harbor. Everyone has a task. Some bailing, some manning the sails, some steering. And everyone has the same task—watching for land.

Then, we notice something through the downpour. Is it a building on the shore? No. It appears to be moving. Perhaps another boat caught in the storm. Let's hope we don't collide.

Then it becomes clearer. It's a figure. A person. Whoever it is appears to be walking on the surface of the water! No one is surprised when we cry out in shock. No one has ever seen such a thing before.

The figure draws closer. It appears to be Jesus. He is walking on the water, the waves of the storm breaking around His knees. And He speaks, "Take courage. It is I. Do not be afraid."[94]

What would you have done? What would you be thinking? What would you be feeling?

Maybe . . .

"We'll be okay; Jesus is coming!"

"He's stilled a storm before, maybe He'll do it again!"[95]

It's easy to read the account. But don't just pass over what we are told.

In the midst of this storm, it would have been nearly impossible to calmly process the idea that Jesus was walking on the water. Because we are familiar with the account, we might not be as startled, as amazed, as those in the boat. It is a nearly incomprehensible sight. And not only has He gained on you in the boat stuck in the middle of the storm, but He also looks like He is going to pass you by. Amazement grips you.

What would you have done then? Storm-tossed, drenched, frightened beyond words, weary. How do you think you would have responded, seeing Jesus walking on the turbulent waves?

ON THE COUNT OF THREE

At that moment, another voice rings out over the winds and the crashing waves. It is Peter. But he doesn't say what we anticipate. He doesn't ask Jesus to stop the storm or help them. He makes an astounding request.

"Jesus, if that is You, command me to come to You on the water."

What?! Peter, what are you thinking? The storm has gotten the best of you.

And then Jesus says, "Come." Peter begins to climb over the side of the boat.

Picture it. This is a fishing boat big enough to hold twelve men in rough seas. Peter has to climb up and over the side of the boat. You are there, holding on, seeking to preserve your life. As you watch Peter lower himself over the side and extend his arms so his feet can come in contact with the water, what is going through your mind?

I can't imagine *not* thinking (or maybe even saying) something like . . .

"This is foolishness!"

"Peter, are you insane? What's with you?"

"Peter, you are going to get yourself killed! You're going to drown!"

"Get back in this boat where it is safe!"

But Peter isn't listening. He's walking on the water. He is stepping, one foot in front of the other, across the surface of the sea. Tentatively at first, but after the first few, a bit more confidently. Jesus is smiling at him through the spray and the wind and the darkness.

Watching him, though, something appears to be going wrong. We can tell Peter is in trouble. He is looking around. He is not far from Jesus now, but clearly something is not right.

Peter is beginning to sink into the water. Jesus is still standing on the surface, the waves lapping at His legs. But we can no longer see Peter's knees. He is slipping into the water. He is beginning to sink.[96]

"I knew it! He's going to get himself killed."

"I told him it was folly!"

"He should have stayed in the boat where it was safe."

As those thoughts run through our minds, Jesus reaches out and takes hold of Peter's hand. Peter had called out, "Command me to come" and Jesus said, "Come!" Now Peter cries out, "Save me!" and Jesus immediately stretches out His hand and takes hold of Peter. He gently pulls, and Peter again rises to the surface. Hand in hand, they make their way back to the boat. As they approach, we can tell they are talking.

Jesus stands on the turbulent water, one hand on the side of the boat, as Peter clambers aboard. Then, Jesus follows. As Jesus gets both feet on the floor of the boat, the wind stops and the rolling eases. The storm has subsided, instantly.

The amazement of what we have just seen is swallowed up in the wonder of Jesus' presence bringing the storm to a standstill. The boat erupts in worship.

It is only later that we get to hear what transpired between the two of them, after Jesus rescued Peter from sinking. Peter tells us. Jesus had said to him, "O little-faithed[97] one, why did you doubt?"

We smile. Because we knew it was a foolish, a stupid thing Peter had done. He should have stayed in the boat, where it was safe. But Peter is not paying much attention to us. As the boat settles in to the shore, he looks back over the sea. Peter is smiling.

I CAN ONLY IMAGINE

There are many amazing things about this miracle. There are many things I turn over and over in my mind and heart.

What was it like to see Jesus walking on the water? How high were the waves? Did the waves come to His knees? Did the men in the boat lose sight of Him in the swells? Things like that cause me to wonder.

But perhaps the thing that amazes me most of all is Jesus' single word, "Come." That staggers me.

I can easily imagine the things the others might have said when Peter asked Jesus to command him to come to Him. I can easily imagine the fears they had, the sense of relatively safety of the boat, and the drama they were watching unfold before them. What I have a hard time imagining is Jesus telling Peter, "Sure! Come on in. The water's fine!" But He does; and Peter does.

I am quick to criticize Peter. I used to think how foolish it was for him to even suggest going out to meet Jesus. I used to think his slipping into the water was merely proof that I was right. He was wrong to even think of doing such a ridiculous thing.

But Jesus apparently didn't think it was ridiculous. After all, He told Peter to come. He wouldn't have done that if He thought it was ridiculous. He wouldn't have called to Peter if He thought it was wrong.

Jesus affirmed Peter's desire to walk on water.

After that experience, Peter would no longer be the same. Think about it: as far as we know, only two people have ever walked on water—Jesus and Peter. But the only reason Peter was able to do it was because he asked Jesus to tell him to come.

We tend to think that this episode reveals a lot about Peter. How foolish he was. Or perhaps how impulsive. We think it shows how wrong he was to step out. It demonstrates how little faith he really had. But I think it tells us something incredible about Jesus.

BETTER SOME THAN NONE

This episode does tell us that Peter had faith. But wait, you say, Jesus rebuked him for his lack of faith. That's partially right. But listen to what Jesus did say.

"O you of little faith, why did you doubt?"

Jesus is not saying Peter had no faith. He is saying that Peter had some faith. He is saying that Peter did trust Him to some degree. The only ones who were entirely lacking in faith were those who remained in the boat. They preferred the safety of wood and nails and sails to the hand of the Son of God.

Peter had enough faith to ask Jesus to command him to come. Enough faith to climb over the side of the boat. Enough faith to take a few steps. And enough faith to cry out to Jesus, knowing He would rescue him. So he had some faith.

In fact, Peter had enough faith to have an adventure with Jesus that no one else has had.

That is amazing. But there is more. There is something here about Jesus.

Jesus is very honest and forthright. He always tells things like they are, even with His closest friends.

Earlier in their journey together, when Peter got out of line suggesting that Jesus might be able to pursue His Messiahship some other way than going to Jerusalem to die, Jesus rebukes Him openly.[98] When the disciples cannot cast a demon out of a small child, Jesus doesn't hesitate to tell them why.[99]

So I must conclude that Jesus wasn't upset or troubled or disappointed or disapproving of Peter's request. If Jesus had been, He either would have said so or He simply would not have called Peter to come for a walk.

This means Jesus must have welcomed Peter's boldness. Even in chastening him for the smallness of his faith, Jesus appreciated Peter's desire to step out in a fresh and radical way to trust Him.

ALL TOO SAFE

I have lived a great deal of my Christian life thinking that Jesus' invitation is a call to grow with Him into a safe, comfortable life. I have mistakenly thought that maturity means less risk, more ease, fewer challenges, more stability. But maybe it's not that way after all.

Maybe Jesus really does want us to step out in fresh adventures with Him. Maybe He really appreciates our asking Him to call us out to risky living and new experiences with Him. Not that we are to be presumptuous. After all, Peter did *ask* Jesus to tell him whether he should come out of the boat or not.

Jesus was not disappointed in Peter. Although He did gently chide Peter for the smallness of his faith, at least Peter was willing to launch out in a new adventure, taking a risk with the One he had come to love and trust. And this acceptance of Peter is evident elsewhere in the Gospels. That Jesus gave Peter a nickname suggests He appreciated Peter's bold, adventurous spirit.

Typically, you give nicknames to those with whom you have a special relationship. And Jesus gave nicknames to three of His disciples—the three who were apparently closest to Him.

On more than one occasion, Jesus took just three of the Twelve with Him. When He went to raise Jairus' daughter from the dead, He took them.[100] On the mount where He was transfigured, they were there.[101] The three were Peter, James, and John. These three were the ones to whom He gave nicknames.

Simon was his name; Jesus gave him the nickname *Peter*. That name means "rock." To the brothers, James and John, Jesus gave the nickname *Sons of Thunder*.

Now when someone was called "son of" something in Jesus' day, it was because there was something about him that stirred such identification.[102] To be a "son of thunder" would mean there was something thunderous about you.

What do we know about these two brothers? Not a lot. But they were the two who wanted to call down fire from heaven on a particular city in Samaria when the residents of that city weren't very welcoming.[103] They are also the two who were scheming as to how they might get the seats of prominence—one on the right, the other on the left—when Jesus came in "power and glory."[104] What we see are two men who were strong-willed, feisty, and bold. That means they were much like Peter.

We know more about Peter than we do about them, though. His bold, jump-in-with-both-feet approach to life and to Jesus is well known. The Gospels are filled with snapshots of Peter's all-in, over-the-top enthusiasm. And he was given a nickname, as well.

Could it be that Jesus embraced these men in an inner circle because there was something He especially appreciated and enjoyed about them? Could it be that Jesus really did want Peter to ask Him if he could come walking on the water? Could it be that Jesus really does want us to give ourselves to Him for bold living, for risk taking, for fresh adventures in faith? Could it be that it was those in the boat, who thought they were safe, who were the ones who missed the adventure of walking on the water with Jesus?

Listening to Jesus' invitation to Peter leads me to wonder if Jesus enjoys inviting His followers into the adventure. Jesus has, through His death and resurrection, brought us into a life we could not have imagined. But He doesn't bring us into this life merely to leave us to live our ordinary human lives. He intends to involve us in His own life—and everything that it might include.

There are lives to touch, bodies needing healing, spiritual forces that must be opposed, messages to proclaim, needs to meet in holy and supernatural ways. And Jesus is going to do those things. And He would like to involve you in those things.

I know that, all too often, I hold back. Stepping into the kind of supernatural ministry Jesus engages in is a bit scary. It takes me beyond myself, beyond what I can pull off. It's like . . . well, it's like walking on water in a storm. Exhilarating, breathtaking, awe-inspiring, frightening, mind-blowing, way out of my comfort zone, and down-right scary stuff. But maybe that's just what Jesus wants for us, for you.

STEPPING INTO OUR ADVENTURE

Each Christian is not called into an identical kind of life. Recognizing this, we might conclude that only some believers get to live lives of great adventures of faith. Maybe such a life is reserved for missionaries and pastors and others we see as extraordinary. Even some people, perhaps, in your local church. But, sadly, so many followers of Jesus settle for lives that are tame and sedate and relatively uninteresting.

Could it be that we are missing out on some of what Jesus wants for us, because we fail to ask? Because we fail to notice Jesus' willingness to invite Peter to walk on water?

James, in his epistle, tells us that sometimes, "you do not have, because you do not ask" (4:2). Peter's cry to Jesus to invite him out of the boat indicates that Peter understood this. If he was going to walk on water with Jesus, he was going to have to ask. So he asked. And he walked on water.

Thinking about this kind of asking, I remember how the church prayed when they faced their first serious persecution (recorded in Acts 4:23-31). After acknowledging God's mastery over all they were experiencing, those believers made some simple, honest requests. They asked the Lord to give them boldness to continue to speak the message of the Gospel; they asked that He would stretch forth His hand and do miraculous things through them. And that is exactly what they received! They asked. And they saw God answer in a powerful way.

I'm not suggesting presumptuously launching off on the most risky and foolhardy thing you can imagine. But I do think that much of my Christian life is filled with prayers for safety and comfort and ease and quietness. Maybe we should be asking for water-walking moments. And when we hear Jesus' call, we need to climb on out of our comfort zone in the storm, and join Jesus in what He is doing.

In one of Paul's prayers for the believers living in Ephesus, he says that God "is able to do exceedingly abundantly beyond all that we ask or think" (Ephesians 3:20). Do you ever think your requests of Jesus are too bold, too extreme? You can trust Him to say "No" if He thinks there is something amiss in your asking. But don't be timid to ask Jesus for adventures in faith, for walking with Him. As He nudges you, as you feel His tug, ask Him. Ask Jesus for true and deep and marvelous experiences with Him. Ask Him to call to you, so you can go walking on the water.

REFLECTING ON THIS TRUTH

FOR PERSONAL REFLECTION:

1. Seeing how willing Jesus is to invite Peter to come walk on the water can help you step into what Jesus wants for you. Talk to Jesus. Ask Him what He wants for you. Ask Him to lead you in fresh ways. Tell Him you are ready for whatever He might have in store for you.

2. Some wonderful and amazing things happen in the lives of those who have walked trustingly with God. Some of these adventures are recorded for us in Hebrews 11. That chapter is no

guarantee that exactly what happened to them will happen to you, but reading that chapter may just encourage you to step out into some fresh venture that Jesus is calling you to. Don't hold back. Whatever He invites you to do, give yourself to it . . . wholeheartedly.

FOR GROUP DISCUSSION:

1. If you had had the opportunity to advise Peter just before he stepped out of the boat, what might you have said to him? Why?

2. What would have kept you from climbing over the side of the boat and joining Jesus in walking on the stormy sea? What would have kept you securely settled in the boat?

3. What is the difference between presumption and trust in Jesus? What do you learn from Peter's experience with Jesus about living in radical dependence and trust?

CHAPTER TEN

WHAT ABOUT THE CRUMBS?

THE WOMAN WITH A DEMONIZED DAUGHTER

But she said, "Yes, Lord; but even the dogs feed on the crumbs which fall from their masters' table."

—Matthew 15:27

A FASCINATING STUDY WAS DONE some years ago to assess the impact of expectations upon perception.[105] The study was elegantly simple. Subjects were briefly shown a series of playing cards and asked to identity them. Included in each series of cards were a few that had been altered: a black three of hearts, a black four of hearts, a red two of spades, a red six of spades, a black ace of diamonds, and a red six of clubs.

Whereas it took almost no time at all for the test subjects to identify the normal cards, it typically took almost four times as long for them to recognize the altered cards. On more than a few occasions, the test subjects ultimately couldn't explain what it was they were seeing.

After a prolonged exposure to one of the altered cards, and feeling frustrated, one test subject said: "I can't make the suit out, whatever it is. It didn't even look like a card that time. I don't know what color it is now or whether it's a spade or heart. I'm not even sure now what a spade looks like!"

What conclusion was drawn from this experiment? Our perception is "powerfully determined by expectations built upon [the] past." And, when expectations are violated (as in seeing something one would not expect to see), the viewer may be unable to even recognize something that is unexpected or incongruous.[106]

To put it simply, when we are confronted with something that doesn't fit with what we expect, our mind resists seeing what is actually there. If the disconnect between what we have come to expect and what is before our eyes is huge, we might not even be able to recognize what we are seeing.

This problem with things "not fitting" can be a challenge in reading Scripture, as well. Our sense of familiarity with a story or passage can set us up with certain expectations. Then when it comes time to give close attention to the passage, there is a tendency to see only what we anticipate seeing. We can leave the accounts only seeing and finding what we expected.

In fact, if the expectations are particularly clear in the mind of the reader, she or he may literally not even be able to see what is in the text. The disconnect between what is expected and what is before the reader, in the text, can make it almost impossible to accept what is right there in plain view in the text.

What can help with this perceptional blindness?

Hold your preconceptions loosely. Of course, no reader can come to a passage without any preunderstanding. We never begin to read with an entirely blank slate. But to diminish the problem of perceptional blindness, it is helpful to admit that we all come with preconceptions and then to choose to hold all such preconclusions loosely. Try to read every text without preassessing what the passage is about.

Pay attention to what is there, in the text. This may seem to go without saying, but it is a critical. Learning to look carefully, to read attentively, to see what the words are genuinely communicating is an underappreciated skill—but something that can be learned. Read as if the one thing that matters is what the text itself actually says.

SHE'S SUCH A BOTHER

Although at first read this story might seem a mix of the familiar—Jesus deals with a demonized person—and the surprising—Jesus appears to be dismissive of the person who is asking for help—there is much more here. The passage before us will provide an opportunity to listen carefully, to draw on preconceived conclusions only minimally, and to learn something fresh about Jesus.

> Jesus went away from there, and withdrew into the district of Tyre and Sidon. And a Canaanite woman from that region came out and began to cry out, saying, "Have mercy on me, Lord, Son of David; my daughter is cruelly

> demon-possessed." But He did not answer her a word. And His disciples came and implored Him, saying, "Send her away, because she keeps shouting at us." But He answered and said, "I was sent only to the lost sheep of the house of Israel." But she came and began to bow down before Him, saying, "Lord, help me!" And He answered and said, "It is not good to take the children's bread and throw it to the dogs." But she said, "Yes, Lord; but even the dogs feed on the crumbs which fall from their masters' table." Then Jesus said to her, "O woman, your faith is great; it shall be done for you as you wish." And her daughter was healed at once.
>
> —Matthew 15:21–28

Matthew provides a lot of details about the woman; we need to give sufficient thought to her. This account is not just about Jesus delivering someone who is oppressed. So let's take a close look at the woman.

She lives in the region of Tyre and Sidon. For many contemporary readers, that might not mean much; for Jesus and the disciples travelling with Him, that would be significant. As you could tell from the maps section of your Bible, Tyre and Sidon are cities on the coast of the Mediterranean Sea, quite a distance north from Palestine. It was a Gentile region. The woman was, most likely, of Gentile birth.

Matthew also tells us she was a "Canaanite."[107] That is more than saying that she was a Gentile; Matthew is identifying her religion of choice. This would mean that the woman—in practice and habit—had been a pagan idolater.

Matthew describes what happened as the woman approached Jesus. She "began to cry out, saying, 'Have mercy on me, Lord, Son of David; my daughter is cruelly demon-possessed.'" The expression "began to cry out" carries more the sense that she continued to cry out. It wasn't a once and done thing. This understanding of her persistence is underscored just a few sentences later when the disciples ask Jesus to send her away because "she *keeps shouting* at us."

When listening to her words, we have to guard against reading too much of our more fully formed New Testament understanding of Jesus into her words. She addresses Jesus as "Lord, Son of David." Does this mean that she is declaring that Jesus is the divine second person of the Trinity come in human flesh to be the atoning sacrifice for the sins of the world? Although those things are all true, it is highly unlikely that this Gentile, pagan woman had such insight—and the language she uses does not force us to conclude that.

To address Jesus as "Lord" may not have had any divine ring to it when the woman spoke to Him. When Christians speak of Jesus as "Lord" and when Paul uses the word in his epistles to refer to Jesus, it is a divine title. But the word can be understood as simply a proper title of respect and deference.[108]

As for addressing Jesus as "Son of David," seeing that the woman was a Canaanite it is not likely that she was thinking in a fully Messianic sense.[109] Although the title "Son of David" would have been a title Jews might use for the promised Messiah, this woman likely did not have enough understanding of the Jewish Scriptures and tradition to have grasped that idea.[110]

So, what is the woman saying in speaking to Jesus as "Lord, Son of David"? It is a respectful cry; minimally it is indicative of her respect for Jesus and her understanding that He is a Jew (in that sense a "son of David"). She recognizes something about Him, even if she doesn't have a fully informed understanding of all He is.

Her repeated entreaty is for Jesus to "have mercy on her" on behalf of her daughter who is cruelly demon-possessed. The woman wants help for her daughter, but she doesn't begin with an appeal for deliverance, but for mercy. And she cried out long enough and persistent enough that the disciples asked Jesus to send her away.

In other words, she is an outsider, she is begging for mercy, and she is making herself a bit of a bother.

WHAT DID HE SAY?

An honest reading of this account confronts me with something startling. Not Jesus' deliverance of a demonized little girl; we know Jesus does that kind of thing. But the exchange Jesus had with the woman—that is surprising and challenging.

The disciples *implored* Jesus to send the woman away—the word suggesting they, like the woman, were persistent in their request. But Jesus did not give in to their demand . . . and apparently He didn't give in to the woman's plea either (at least not immediately).

Jesus said—in apparent response to both the disciples and the woman—"I was sent only to the lost sheep of the house of Israel."

How would the disciples, and the woman, have heard this? What would it mean to them?

Having been with Jesus for some time now, the disciples would have at least understood that Jesus was underscoring His ministry to the Jewish people. That is where He has spent most of His time.[111] They might have understood His remark to be a bit dismissive of the woman. "Good! He's going to send her away!" might have been their initial conclusion. It's also hard not to conclude that the woman may have heard these words as somewhat dismissive. After all, she is a Gentile and a Canaanite; she hardly qualifies as one of the "lost sheep of the house of Israel."[112]

But the woman persisted—I can almost hear the groan from the lips of the disciples as the woman continues to cry out. She reasserted her request—and this time she began to bow down before Him, the idea being that she kept on crying out to Jesus from a kneeling posture.[113] As we have seen with others who have come to Jesus, she is desperate; she is abandoning herself to Him in the hope of receiving some help.

As she continued to beg, Jesus addressed her directly. What I hear from Jesus' lips sounds like one of the harshest things He ever said to anyone: "And He answered and said, 'It is not good to take the children's bread and throw it to the dogs.'"

In Jesus' day, Jews might refer to Gentiles as "dogs." It was believed that Gentiles were outside the covenant God had with His people, that they were not heirs to God's promises to the patriarchs, that they were corrupt in their religious practices. So the Jews looked down on the Gentiles, and "dogs" was considered an appropriate way to refer to them.[114]

But Jesus did not use the simple word for *dog*; He used the diminutive form—"little dogs."[115] Although Jesus was using what would have been understood as a common cultural metaphor in referring to Israel as the children and Gentiles as dogs, He seems to be softening the image a bit. So what is He doing?

The woman's response points us in the right direction. "But she said, 'Yes, Lord; but even the dogs feed on the crumbs which fall from their masters' table.'"

WHAT DID SHE SAY?

The woman began with two words that should always go together: "Yes, Lord." Her regard for Jesus (even though she likely didn't fully understand who He was) left her affirming what He said: "Yes, what You say is right."

Jesus' statement about not taking the children's bread and giving it to dogs must be understood as saying something about His mission. He is not going to turn away from His primary call—proclaiming the good news to the nation of Israel. And even though this woman is desperate for His mercy to bring help to her daughter, she readily affirms that what Jesus wants is the right thing.

She follows up this simple affirmation with a wonderful counterpoint to Jesus' remarks. "Yes, Lord; but even the dogs feed on the crumbs which fall from their masters' table." Building on Jesus' own language, the woman continues to plead her case. But how she pleads her case is critical.

Having confessed that she understands Jesus' mission and affirming that she sees His call to give "bread" to the "children," she offers a metaphor that captures what she longs for . . . and what she anticipates from Jesus. She simply says, "I'll be happy with crumbs from Your table."

If Jesus' words were startling, the woman's response is amazing. Jesus affirms just how amazing in declaring that her faith is "great"[116] and that what she was longing for—the deliverance of her daughter—will be done.

Did she corner Jesus? Was she able to get Jesus to change His mind and do what she wanted Him to do after all . . . even after having received a rebuff? Was this about the woman winning out over Jesus? Unlikely. But how then do we make sense of their exchange . . . and the result?

Jesus affirmed His personal mission and clarified that He wasn't going to abandon that to help her. The woman agreed that what He said was right and proper, but then asserted that she would be grateful for any scrap of grace He might be willing to extend to her.

She asked for mercy—gracious kindness. She laid herself out at Jesus' feet—begging for help. She made it clear that she had no intention of derailing Jesus' plans—she affirmed what He wanted was right. And she anticipated that mere "crumbs" from Jesus would be sufficient for whatever need she had.

This Gentile, pagan woman with only limited familiarity with Jesus was so convinced of the kind of man that He was that she was certain that crumbs from the table He was setting was better than anything she could find elsewhere. We are not told how she learned about Jesus or much of what she understood about His identity, but we are clearly shown that she was ready to abandon herself to His grace and mercy.

WILL I SETTLE FOR THE CRUMBS?

Having walked with Jesus for years and obviously having a more informed view of who He is than did this woman, I am sad to say that at times I still struggle to affirm that I would be willing to take the crumbs that Jesus allows to fall my way. I don't often share in this woman's confidence in the goodness of His freely extended grace.

In my times of need, I typically approach Jesus with a clear agenda—my agenda, and not His. I want Him to do specific things in particular ways at a prescribed time with a predetermined outcome. I am not suggesting that we can't come to Jesus with such items on our agenda. But it does seem to me that when I do approach Jesus this way I am not wholly trusting, not fully depending, not completely believing in Him to the degree that this woman did.

For this woman, it is Jesus' mercy, Jesus' help, Jesus' plan, Jesus' priorities, Jesus' crumbs. She would be satisfied with whatever He wanted to bestow. And what she received from Him was remarkable and needed . . . and entirely consistent with Jesus' gracious character.

There is an appropriate tension between coming to Jesus with our needs with a specific end in mind (as the leper did[117]) and coming to Jesus as this woman did, with a willingness to receive from Jesus whatever He wishes to give. There are times in life where either approach is fitting. But do we ever get to the place where we share in the woman's great faith and willingly settle for crumbs from Jesus?

It seems that Paul, the apostle, learned how to live there—in the "crumbs are more than sufficient" kind of life with Jesus. Paul had been gloriously led into both truths and experiences of the good news about Jesus—he was the recipient of revelations and a servant of God who exercised great power through the Spirit. But he also knew about "crumbs are sufficient" living. Writing to the church in Corinth, he explained:

> Because of the surpassing greatness of the revelations, for this reason, to keep me from exalting myself, there was given me a thorn in the flesh, a messenger of Satan to torment me—to keep me from exalting myself! Concerning this I implored the Lord three times that it might leave me. And He has said to me, "My grace is sufficient for you, for power is perfected in weakness." Most gladly, therefore, I will rather boast about my weaknesses, so that the power of Christ may dwell in me. Therefore I am well content with weaknesses, with insults, with distresses, with persecutions, with difficulties, for Christ's sake; for when I am weak, then I am strong.
>
> —2 Corinthians 12:7–10

Paul repeatedly approached Jesus with his need. So did the woman. Paul begged Jesus for help. So did the woman. Paul recognized that His grace is sufficient—whatever Jesus chose to grant in the moment of need would be more than enough. So did the woman.

Adopting such a perspective isn't a game to play. We shouldn't pretend that we will settle for crumbs when all along we are insistent on something more. We shouldn't claim we will be content with grace while what we truly mean is that we question whether Jesus will do what is good and right and beneficial if we don't inform Him of what should be done. This miracle provides us with a vivid picture—seen in the woman and confirmed in Paul—of what is at the heart of great faith.

We need to see Jesus as so great and kind and gracious and wise and good and powerful that it makes sense to our hearts and minds to say, "Whatever You decide would be good to do in this moment of need is all that I ask. That will be enough."

REFLECTING ON THIS TRUTH

FOR PERSONAL REFLECTION:

1. This woman, even with her incomplete view of Jesus, apparently saw Him as someone she could trust with her greatest struggles. Spend some time reflecting on what you know about Jesus. Don't focus so much on what you would like Him to do, just spend time celebrating what you know to be true about Him.

2. What do you do when you feel your needs are too much for you? How do you approach Jesus when you are feeling overwhelmed? The Canaanite woman came with a definite disposition of dependency—she ceaselessly asked, she prostrated herself before Jesus, she affirmed that His plans were always right. When was the last time you expressed such heartfelt and unreserved dependency on Jesus? What holds you back from that kind of full abandonment to Him?

3. This woman's glad confession that she would happily take "the crumbs" from the hand of Jesus was a sincere confession of faith. Those words did not force Jesus to act, but they were an admission that she was willing to receive whatever He might want to grant her. Not insisting that Jesus do a particular thing in a specific way frees us up to more readily receive from Him what He wants to do—something that will always be good and gracious and beneficial. Throughout the day, talk with Jesus and let Him know that you are quite glad to receive from Him whatever He chooses to pour into your life.

FOR GROUP DISCUSSION:

1. Describe the situation as it first unfolds. Where is Jesus? Who is with Him? What would it have been like to have this woman break into the group and begin calling out to Him?

2. Why do you think the disciples wanted Jesus to dismiss the woman? Can you see yourself responding the way they did? Why or why not?

3. Jesus' affirmation of the greatness of the woman's faith must have had some impact on the disciples' thinking. In that moment, hearing those words, what might they have thought? How does this exchange between the woman and Jesus nudge you to be more dependent on Jesus and His grace?

CHAPTER ELEVEN

I THOUGHT IT WAS ABOUT THEM

THE FEEDING OF THE MULTITUDE

But He answered them, "You give them something to eat!" And they said to Him, "Shall we go and spend two hundred denarii on bread and give them something to eat?"

—Mark 6:37

I CAN STILL REMEMBER ONE night on the island of Eleuthera. I was with a short-term mission team on that island, working with an organization that was training Bahamian church leaders. The day had been well spent, and we were all pretty exhausted. We went to the top of the hill above the center where we were staying. We stretched out on a concrete slab there. Our tired backs felt the warmth of the sun that the cement had absorbed during the day. And we looked up.

It was a crystal-clear evening. There is almost no light pollution on Eleuthera. It was deep dark all around us, but the sky was brilliant with countless stars. Breathtaking! For the longest time, no one spoke. It was an incredible vista. So many stars!

It's not that those countless stars weren't always there—even back home. They are ceaseless sentinels, patrolling the night sky each evening. But at home, the lights of the world around us blind us from seeing the stars. It was the distractionless Bahamian night sky that aided us in seeing what we never did see well at home.

In other words, even at home we have the capacity to see the stars, given the right situation, the best conditions.

Did you know that it takes some time for your eyes even to see in the dark? The way the eye processes light requires a period of time for everything to get set for you to maximize your vision in a dark environment. If you step outside, from your well-lit house out onto the back porch and wander away from the lighted patio, you will be able to see some stars. But if you stay out in the dark for half an hour, you will be able to see considerably more stars than when you first glanced up to the sky.[118]

Some evenings, however, it's hard to even see the moon. The clouds interfere with your line of sight. Trees and buildings obscure the view. Even on a clear night, standing on the streets of a small town, looking up into the night sky, you might not be able to see many stars. It's not that they're not there. It's just that the ambient light spilling into your field of vision hides their brilliance.

Do you want to see the stars better? Without having to book a trip to Eleuthera? Even standing on the street where you live? Grab a cardboard tube from a roll of paper towels; better yet, the longer tube from a roll of wrapping paper. Cover or close one eye and look through the tube with the other. Scan the sky. You'll be surprised at what you can now see. The tube diminishes the impact of the light pollution and helps you focus on those white-hot markers in the heavens.

That is what I'm hoping happens in these reflections on Jesus' miracles. There are marvelous, brilliant, breathtaking things recorded for us in these Gospel accounts. But sometimes what is there is obscured. The way we've heard the stories taught, what we think Jesus is trying to communicate, what we think matters most, can obscure the view and get in the way. Our ambient thoughts—a kind of "reading pollution"—that spills into our minds and hearts as we read the accounts can hide the brilliance of what Jesus is revealing.

So let's block out the extraneous words and those troubling ambient thoughts and focus our attention on one well known and, perhaps, little understood miracle of Jesus.

IT HAD BEEN A BUSY FEW WEEKS

Jesus had gathered a band of men around Himself; twelve in total. His purpose? To have them share life with Him so they could, eventually, do the same kinds of things that He Himself was doing.[119] After spending many months together, Jesus sent them out with a particular commission; they were given an assignment to share the message Jesus was proclaiming and to demonstrate the validity of that message in how they ministered to those in need.[120]

For these apostles,[121] those days "out in the field" would have been busy, challenging, eye-opening, and compelling. They have now returned to Jesus, having finished their initial "short-term mission trip." And it is upon their return that we pick up the account.

> The apostles gathered together with Jesus; and they reported to Him all that they had done and taught. And He said to them, "Come away by yourselves to a secluded place and rest a while." (For there were many people coming and going, and they did not even have time to eat.) They went away in the boat to a secluded place by themselves. The people saw them going, and many recognized them and ran there together on foot from all the cities, and got there ahead of them.
>
> When Jesus went ashore, He saw a large crowd, and He felt compassion for them because they were like sheep without a shepherd; and He began to teach them many things. When it was already quite late, His disciples came to Him and said, "This place is desolate and it is already quite late; send them away so that they may go into the surrounding countryside and villages and buy themselves something to eat." But He answered them, "You give them something to eat!" And they said to Him, "Shall we go and spend two hundred denarii[122] on bread and give them something to eat?"
>
> And He said to them, "How many loaves do you have? Go look!" And when they found out, they said, "Five, and two fish." And He commanded them all to sit down by groups on the green grass. They sat down in groups of hundreds and of fifties. And He took the five loaves and

> the two fish, and looking up toward heaven, He blessed the food and broke the loaves and He kept giving them to the disciples to set before them; and He divided up the two fish among them all. They all ate and were satisfied, and they picked up twelve full baskets of the broken pieces, and also of the fish. There were five thousand men who ate the loaves.
>
> —Mark 6:30–44

If we run too quickly to the end of the story—only focusing on the size of the group that was fed and being duly impressed with that—we could miss other important pieces. If we let things we've been told or heard about this miracle hide what Mark wants to communicate, we might not see what he wants his readers to see. Let's not allow any mental "light pollution" to obscure the brightness of what is here, in the passage.

The best way to minimize such distractions is to focus on the words of the text. (Grab a cardboard tube if it helps!) Reading the passage as if everything we need to know is right there.

This account begins with the apostles' regathering to Jesus and His words to them. He wants to take them somewhere secluded so that they can rest. Apparently, with the extension of Jesus' ministry through the Twelve, the crowds have continued to grow. There are now so many people and so many needs and so much commotion that they "did not even have time to eat."

Mark does not tell us what Jesus' disciples understood by His invitation, but they must have anticipated some change of pace from what they had been doing as they got into the boat with Him.

The lake of Galilee is not a large body of water; there are villages sprinkled all around the edges of the lake. As Jesus and the disciples headed out in a boat, the crowds who had been following Jesus (and, probably, some who had received ministry at the hands of the apostles) noticed the departure. So they started around the lake, anticipating where Jesus and the Twelve might disembark. Think of it as a large, loosely-organized, spontaneous marathon. By the time Jesus and the disciples disembarked, the crowd they were leaving behind had already assembled in anticipation.

I can almost hear the discouragement in the voices of the disciples as they get out of the boat with Jesus on the far side of the lake. "We were hoping to get away! Where did this huge crowd come from?" But Jesus' response to the crowd is different; He sees them in their neediness. They need "shepherding," so Jesus begins to teach them.

MY STOMACH IS GROWLING

We don't know exactly how long Jesus taught the crowd, but we do know that it ran long enough that the disciples' stomachs probably started to growl. They saw the need to send the crowd away so the people could forage for something to eat.

On the surface of it, what they asked of Jesus seems reasonable. The Twelve had just returned from an adventure where they were not allowed to take anything with them. The only thing they had to eat was what was provided for them by others. They weren't permitted to take money with them. And now they are out in an unpopulated area, without resources or any recourse for provisions. So their request makes sense. "Send the people away so that they can get themselves something to eat." I'm pretty sure I would have been thinking the same thing, had I been in their situation.

Undoubtedly, Jesus' response—"you give all these people something to eat"—caught them by surprise. This is clear from their reaction to Him: the disciples balked. I think there must have been at least a hint of sarcasm in how they responded. "Yeah, sure! We—whom You told to carry nothing with us as we journeyed—we will just pool our resources, come up with the equivalent of nearly a year's wages, and go to the corner market here in this unpopulated area and buy box dinners for everyone. What a great idea!" Although I'd like to think I would have responded without even a hint of sarcasm, I doubt I would have found Jesus' suggestion very reasonable.

Seeing as the disciples were unclear how they should follow through on Jesus' instructions, He gave them the particulars. The food on hand was gathered—a meager five loaves and two fish.[123] The crowd was sorted and seated. Then something remarkable happened.

I have often wondered how this particular miracle played out. As I read the text, a couple of things stand out to me that help me imagine what it might have been like.

The verb tenses are suggestive. (Something a good English translation does help us with.) Jesus "*took* the loaves . . . and the fish." That's a simple past tense.[124] "*Looking up* to heaven" is a participle form; it points to something that is coterminous with the main action. In this case, the "looking up" goes with the *blessing* and *breaking* of the bread. Both those verbs are also simple past tenses. What is fascinating is how Mark describes the distribution of the food.

Jesus *"kept giving* [the broken bread] to the disciples" to give it to the people. Here there is a change in verb tense. The way the language works, this tells us that the miracle was actually happening in Jesus' hands. He kept on continually breaking the bread, and there continued to be more to break.

Mark writes that there were five thousand men at this picnic. That's a typical way for a Jew in Jesus' day to count a group: the number of men. Estimates are that there could have been as many as 15,000, counting women and children.

So if Jesus kept breaking and kept on giving the bread to the disciples and the disciples were then wandering out into the crowd of ten or fifteen thousand, who saw what was happening? Do you think the people out in the cheap seats genuinely grasped all that was going on? Or is it more likely that the Twelve were the only ones who actually saw the miracle?

DINNER'S OVER, TIME TO CLEAN UP

After the crowd is fed, the disciples gather up the remains. Twelve baskets full; one for each of the disciples. Jesus sent His disciples away in the boat they came in while He remained to dismiss the others.[125]

So we are left with an amazing miracle. Thousands fed with five loaves and two fish. But that leaves me with a question: What of it? What was it all about?

Did you notice? Before when Jesus healed someone, there was often amazement.[126] But here we get no report of a response—other than everyone ate and was satisfied. Was this because the crowd didn't fully grasp what had happened? Perhaps. But maybe the reason there was no response from the crowd is because the miracle wasn't, fundamentally, for them.

The first hint that this miracle was not primarily about the crowd is seen in the twelve baskets full of scraps that were gathered. Clearly, those baskets were for the twelve disciples; the scraps weren't distributed to the crowd to take home.

The next thing to note is what prompted the miracle. This moment starts with an exchange between Jesus and the disciples. There is something going on between them that needs to be resolved. Perhaps the miracle is where the resolution comes.

The last indicator of what this miracle is all about comes a few verses later where we read that the disciples had "hard hearts" and that they "had not gained any insight from the incident of the loaves" (Mark 6:52). This must mean that the "incident of the loaves" was not simply about feeding a hungry crowd, but about teaching the disciples something. With that in mind, let's revisit the exchanges Jesus had with His Twelve to see if we can uncover what He wanted them to see.

We begin with the last words of Jesus to the Twelve: "You give them something to eat." As you recall, they bristled at the idea. Their less-than-polite answer tells us that they couldn't conceive of doing that. But what ultimately happened? Jesus kept giving the disciples the food, and they did, in fact, give the food to the people. What Jesus wanted for them—to give the people something to eat—is exactly what happened. It just didn't play out the way that these disciples likely imagined it would.

But Jesus meant what He said to them. The problem was they didn't take what He said to heart. Instead, they were a bit dismissive. But this isn't the only moment when they may not have taken seriously what He had said.

This episode opened with Jesus words to them: "Come away by yourselves to a secluded place and rest a while." If we listen carefully, it becomes evident that all of these words of Jesus did come to pass . . . but the twelve may not have listened well to these words.

"Come away by yourselves . . ." The disciples did go away by themselves with Jesus; they left in the boat alone. It just happened that when they got to their destination, others had run ahead to meet them there. But they did go away by themselves.

"Come away . . . to a secluded place . . ." He told them they were going to a "secluded" place. When the disciples asked to have the crowd sent away, they affirmed they were indeed in just such a place. Although they were now there with people, nevertheless the place qualified as secluded, or desolate.[127]

"Come away . . . to rest a while . . ." It's this part of Jesus' call that may leave us a bit puzzled. He called them away to "rest a while." Was that invitation fulfilled? It is this question that points the way forward to understand what was going on in what Jesus wanted for the Twelve.

PALM TREES AND AN OCEAN BREEZE

How would you have heard the invitation to rest a while? After the adventure the disciples had been on in ministering to others, I think I might have heard those words as a call to find myself on a nice beach, swinging lazily in a hammock, the refreshing breeze wafting through the trees, while I sipped on something cool brought to me by a kind and dutiful servant.

When the teaching time was through, and the day was getting late, the disciples proposed that Jesus send the crowd away. They wanted to rest. They wanted to solve the problem of the crowd's need by having the people go find food for themselves. Yet Jesus wanted to solve the problem by having the Twelve respond to the need.[128]

I wonder if what causes the glitch in the disciples' thinking (and their resultant "hardness of heart") is the apparent discrepancy between how they understood Jesus' call to come away and rest and what they heard in Jesus' words "you give them something to eat."

If they understood Jesus' call to rest as if it were an invitation to idleness and inactivity, then His subsequent call to give the crowd something to eat would have been incongruent. Those two ideas wouldn't go together. And if they were sold on the idea of just putting up their feet and doing nothing, they easily could have been put out by Jesus' call to give food to the multitude. This might explain the subsequent hardness of heart. It arose from the intersection of "I want to rest" and "providing food for the masses doesn't look like rest!"

But this conflict in thought only arises if they understood "rest" as "cessation of labor." The only other time this word is used by Mark is when the disciples are "resting" in the Garden while Jesus is praying.[129] In that passage, it might indicate cessation of labor, but that passage might not be conclusive for our understanding of what is going on in the feeding. There is another passage that might point us toward what Jesus meant by "come . . . and rest."

Jesus, speaking to His followers, explained: "Come to Me, all who are weary and heavy-laden, and I will give you rest. Take my yoke upon you and learn from Me, for I am gentle and humble of heart, and you will find rest for your souls" (Matthew 11:28–29).

In this passage from Matthew, Jesus uses the same language as that found in the feeding story. Jesus invites His followers to come with Him. And in both passages He promises rest. But the "rest" here, in this passage from Matthew, cannot mean a cessation of labor because it includes taking up a yoke (suggesting a task to be done) and learning from Jesus (which points to attentive growing understanding).

Could it be that when Jesus invited the disciples to rest in the feeding account, He was calling them to take up a yoke and learn from Him? That He was *not* calling them to sit back and not do anything? Their weariness from the ministry they had been doing on their own was to be alleviated by a definite dependence upon Jesus as they rejoined Him.

Maybe the invitation to rest was not inconsistent with the call to give the people something to eat. The call to respond to the massive need they were facing was not a command for the Twelve to do something about it on their own (which is how they understood the call to give the people something to eat). It was an invitation to greater reliance upon Jesus; to more fully lean on and attend to Him so as to learn what He wanted to do about the need. Jesus didn't want them to figure out how to meet the need of the multitude but to depend on Him more; Jesus wasn't asking them to provide the resources to feed the many, but to realize more fully how to look to Him.

RESTING WHILE LABORING

Apparently, the Twelve were thinking something like this:

> Jesus intends for us to go to a secluded place to rest.
>
> Whew! We got to the secluded place.
>
> Wow! There is a massive need here.
>
> When? When will He be done talking to them?
>
> What? Jesus now intends for us to meet that need?
>
> How? We don't have the means to meet such a need in ourselves!
>
> What happened to our rest?

What Jesus really wanted for them would require thinking more along these lines:

> Jesus intends for us to join Him in a secluded place to rest.
>
> Whew! This is a secluded place.
>
> Wow! Jesus still wants to meet the need of the people.
>
> When? When will He be done with them?
>
> What? He intends for them to be fed . . . and He wants to involve us?

> How? We won't be able to do this without resting on Him. I wonder what He wants to do.
>
> We will have to rest!

If we think along these lines, we end up concluding that this miracle was not so much about the meeting of the need of the multitude—it was the occasion for a lesson for the Twelve. If we think along these lines, we can make sense of the statement that they "had not learned anything from the incident of the loaves"—which tells us that the feeding was for their training and not merely to provide miracle bread for the multitude.

In one sense, we could say that they simply misunderstood. They thought the feeding of the multitude was about the crowd. But it wasn't. It was about them, about what Jesus wanted them to learn.

Realizing this, we can make sense of another fascinating clue about the meaning of this miracle—it happens to be the one specific miracle Jesus repeats[130] and, in repeating the miracle, He asks His disciples if they "yet understand."[131] It would seem that Jesus thought the miracle of the feeding of the multitude was really a lesson in learning for the Twelve.

WHAT IF IT'S NOT ABOUT "THEM"?

I realize that as Jesus involves me in what He is doing in the lives of others I can fall into the same kind of misunderstandings that plagued the Twelve in this account. If I am not careful, I can miss what He wants me to see and, in my hard-heartedness, overlook what He is teaching me.

Like the Twelve, my misunderstanding arises from two things:

I understand that Jesus invites me to join Him, but I mistakenly think He intends me to come up with the resources to meet the need.

I understand Jesus' call to rest, but I mistakenly think it means He doesn't want me to participate with Him in meeting the need.

I hear Jesus' invitation to do life with Him. I do understand that there is a rest I can find with Him. Yet when He subsequently calls my attention to some need, I balk.

One of those moments for me came some years ago, when a man set up an appointment for some marriage counseling. Our first meeting was just the two of us; his wife did not attend. He shared his need. And it was overwhelming.

He and his wife were both struggling with alcoholism. It wasn't the first marriage for either of them. They had both gotten drunk on their honeymoon. Trying to help her back to the hotel after she had passed out in the car, he had accidentally dropped her. She was jarred alert and accused him of beating her up. Now he had a pending charge of criminal domestic violence. And he wanted me to help them. As I was stumbling along, trying to keep up with all he was telling me, I asked about what he did for a living. He explained that he was an addictions counselor.

And I thought: I don't have the resources to deal with this! Jesus can't expect me to get involved here!

And I thought: Jesus wants me to rest in Him! He can't be intending for me to step into this situation!

But I was wrong. In grace, Jesus didn't leave me in my hard-heartedness. He led me and taught me and showed me and provided the needed resources. He gave me His grace so that I could rest in Him. And miracles followed. Lives were changed. And it was all His doing. It wasn't about them; it was about what Jesus wanted to teach me.

Maybe that call He has given you—to repair a relationship, to serve in a new way, to give resources and time beyond what you think possible, to extend forgiveness, to fill a new position at work—maybe that call is not about the others. Maybe it is about what He would like to teach you.

Certainly, the needs of others might be met. Yes, there might be a miraculous display of His power and grace. But it could just be that all of that is for you to learn something about Him—something you would not have seen if He hadn't called you to "come and rest" and then to participate with Him in something you could never conceive of doing on your own.

REFLECTING ON THIS TRUTH

FOR PERSONAL REFLECTION:

1. Can you hear yourself responding to Jesus and speaking to Jesus the way the Twelve did in this account? Why or why not? What do you see in yourself that is like them? What do you see that you feel is different?

2. Look around in your life at the situations and relationships that Jesus has placed you into. Do you ever feel overwhelmed by the needs? Do you ever see yourself as inadequate for addressed the needs? In feeding the multitude, Jesus is not asking for either the disciples' plans or the disciples' resources. He only wanted

their availability. How could seeing that move you forward in connecting with the needs that He alerts you to in the lives of those around you?

3. What would it look like, in the midst of the various demands you feel pulling at you, for you to rest in Jesus? If you realized that responding to Jesus' call to rest is not a call to inactivity, how might you approach life's challenges differently? Talk with Him about what He is calling you to, and how you could rest in responding to that invitation.

FOR GROUP DISCUSSION:

1. As you read and think through this account, try to not be too hard on the disciples; see them as real people facing some huge challenges. How do you imagine you might have responded: like they did? Differently than they did?

2. If the Twelve had understood Jesus' invitation to "rest" to be more about dependency on Him rather than merely the absence of any labor, how might they have responded to His call for them to give something to the multitude to eat?

3. Everything Jesus had said to the Twelve came to pass: coming away, the secluded place, the rest, and the giving of food to the multitude. How does realizing that encourage you in your journey with Jesus, as you listen to what He says to you?

CHAPTER TWELVE

IT'S WHO YOU KNOW

THE RAISING OF LAZARUS

So Jesus said to them plainly, "Lazarus is dead, and I am glad for your sakes that I was not there, so that you may believe; but let us go to him."

—John 11:14–15

I REMEMBER HEARING A STORY about a country cousin visiting his relative in New York City. As the two of them walked near Times Square, the young man who had grown up in the country stopped and said, "Wait, I think I hear a cricket."

The city-living cousin asked incredulously, "You can hear a cricket in the midst of all this noise and hustle and bustle? You've got to be kidding me."

In response, the other began looking around, insisting he had heard a cricket. A few moments later he found it at the base of tree on the sidewalk. Retrieving the cricket, he presented it to the city-dweller.

"How were you able to hear that?" came the question.

In reply, the country cousin reached into his pocket and pulled out a bunch of change. "Just watch." He dumped the change on the sidewalk.

Dozens of people who were in the midst of jostling one another in pursuit of their individual mission across the concrete, immediately stopped. Heads turned. Attention was captured by the sound of the coins hitting the ground.

"I guess it's a matter of what you are accustomed to listen for. We hear what we are tuned in to hear."

That can happen when we read Biblical texts as well. We will watch for and pick up on the things we are tuned in to find. If we are not careful readers, we will find only what we have already concluded the text before us is about.

We've seen this as we have worked through a number of Jesus' miracles. If we read the accounts assuming that they simply are proofs of Jesus' divinity, we tend to find only that. The more impressive the miracle and the more familiar the story, the easier it is to listen only for what we have been told the story is all about. We end up not hearing other things—other critical things—in the story.

Even many of those who are not regular church attendees know the basic story we are looking at in this chapter—the raising of Lazarus from the dead. Those familiar with the story conclude that this account really is about proving that Jesus, having the power of life and death, is God. There's no reason to deny that truth. But what is so interesting about the account is that John takes forty-four verses to tell us the story—many more words, surely, than John would need to simply tell us that Jesus was God, evidenced by His raising a dead man to life.[132]

The question is whether there is something more in the account we need to be listening for. We need to lean in and notice the other elements of John's account—elements that tell us some wonderful things about how Jesus wants us to relate to Him.

I'VE GOT A BAD FEELING ABOUT THIS

After years of walking with Jesus and through many hours studying the Gospels, I have come to the conclusion that Jesus doesn't often do things the way I think He should. After Jesus had healed a large number of people gathered at Simon's mother-in-law's house, the next morning He arose to pray and ultimately left a number of people unhealed at the house.[133] I would have recommended that Jesus go back. When Jesus was on His way to Jairus' house to heal the man's daughter, He took time to listen to the whole story of the woman who was healed of her flow of blood.[134] I would have urged him to come back to her (if necessary) and instead to hurry up and attend to Jairus' dying daughter. On quite a number of occasions, I think I would have advised Jesus to do things differently than I find recorded in the Gospels.

I feel this tug to offer advice when I read through the account we're looking at in this chapter. I can think of a number of suggestions that would have altered the way things played out and would have circumvented the "problem" of Lazarus' seemingly untimely death. But I have come to understand that if I had my way, what Jesus intended to reveal about Himself would have been lost. With that, let's turn to the account.

Now a certain man was sick, Lazarus of Bethany, of the village of Mary and her sister Martha. And it was the Mary who anointed the Lord with ointment, and wiped His feet with her hair, whose brother Lazarus was sick. The sisters therefore sent to Him, saying, "Lord, behold, he whom You love is sick."[135]

But when Jesus heard it, He said, "This sickness is not unto death, but for the glory of God, that the Son of God may be glorified by it."[136]

Now Jesus loved Martha, and her sister, and Lazarus. When therefore He heard that he was sick, He stayed then two days longer in the place where He was. Then after this He said to His disciples, "Let us go to Judea again. Our friend, Lazarus has fallen asleep; but I go, that I may awaken him out of sleep."

The disciples therefore said to Him, "Lord, if he has fallen asleep, he will recover."

Now Jesus had spoken of his death; but they thought that He was speaking of literal sleep. Then Jesus therefore said to them plainly, "Lazarus is dead, and I am glad for your sake that I was not there, so that you may believe; but let us go to him."

So when Jesus came, He found that Lazarus had already been in the tomb four days. Now Bethany was near Jerusalem, about two miles off; and many of the Jews had come to Martha and Mary, to console them concerning their brother.

Martha therefore, when she heard that Jesus was coming, went to meet Him; but Mary still sat in the house. Martha therefore said to Jesus, "Lord, if You had been here, my brother would not have died. Even now I know that whatever You ask of God, God will give You."

Jesus said to her, "Your brother shall rise again."

Martha said to Him, "I know that he will rise again in the resurrection on the last day."[137]

Jesus said to her, "I am the resurrection and the life; he who believes in Me shall live even if he dies, and everyone who lives and believes in Me shall never die. Do you believe this?"

She said to Him, "Yes, Lord; I have believed that You are the Christ, the Son of God, even He who comes into the world." And when she had said this, she went away, and called Mary her sister, saying secretly, "The Teacher is here, and is calling for you." And when she heard it, she arose quickly, and was coming to Him.

Now Jesus had not yet come into the village, but was still in the place where Martha met Him. The Jews then who were with her in the house, and consoling her, when they saw that Mary rose up quickly and went out, followed her, supposing that she was going to the tomb to weep there.

Therefore, when Mary came where Jesus was, she saw Him, and fell at His feet, saying to Him, "Lord, if You had been here, my brother would not have died."

When Jesus therefore saw her weeping, and the Jews who came with her, also weeping, He was deeply moved in spirit, and was troubled, and said, "Where have you laid him?" They said to Him, "Lord, come and see." Jesus wept. And so the Jews were saying, "Behold how He loved him!" But some of them said, "Could not this man, who opened the eyes of him who was blind, have kept this man also from dying?"[138]

Jesus therefore again being deeply moved within, came to the tomb. Now it was a cave, and a stone was lying against it. Jesus said, "Remove the stone."

Martha, the sister of the deceased, said to Him, "Lord, by this time there will be a stench; for he has been dead four days."

Jesus said to her, "Did I not say to you, if you believe, you will see the glory of God?" And so they removed the stone.

And Jesus raised His eyes, and said, "Father, I thank You that You heard Me. And I know that You hear me always; but because of the people standing around I said it, that they may believe that You did send Me." And when He had said these things, He cried out with a loud voice, "Lazarus, come forth."

> He who had died came forth, bound hand and foot with wrappings; and his face was wrapped around with a cloth. Jesus said to them, "Unbind him, and let him go."
>
> —John 11:1–44

Why does Jesus wait before going to see Lazarus? John wrote, "When therefore [Jesus] heard that he was sick, He stayed then two days longer in the place where He was." At first read, that doesn't make any sense to me. Hearing that Lazarus was sick, Jesus decided to wait. That seems to be anything but attentive and caring. I would have encouraged Jesus to go to Lazarus as soon as He heard of his need. But Jesus apparently sees things differently.

Earlier in John's Gospel, Jesus explained that He did only the things He saw the Father doing (John 5:19–20). Minimally, this must mean that when Jesus says He knows Lazarus' illness is not "unto death" but that the Father is going to get glory through this, He has been in communication with the Father about what is going on. The Father has a plan, Jesus is in on it, and we are going to watch it unfold.[139]

And what is that plan? Hearing that Lazarus was sick and knowing what He knows, Jesus stays two days longer. To get the timing clearly in mind, let's do a little math around those two days.

It was a one-day trip from where Jesus was, across the Jordan, to Bethany (John10:40). So the servant of Martha and Mary makes a one-day trip to find and call on Jesus. Jesus decides to wait two days before making the return trip back to Bethany. He takes a day to get there. When He arrives we are told that Lazarus has been buried for four days. In that place and time the dead were buried as soon as possible because the conditions were ripe for speedy decomposition. That being the case, Lazarus might well have died before the servant reached Jesus to tell Him Lazarus was ill. Jesus apparently knew this. After all, before going (and without any other word from Bethany) He tells His disciples, "Lazarus is dead."

He already knew Lazarus was dead. He knew He wasn't going to Bethany to simply heal a sick man. He waited, knowing that Lazarus would be "good and dead" by the time He got there.

Don't miss this. Jesus told His disciples why He was doing this, why He waited, why He was not going until after Lazarus was dead. "I am glad for your sake that I was not there, so that you may believe."

Does Jesus mean by this that He was glad He wasn't going to just heal a sick friend but actually to raise a dead man so His disciples would come to a correct theological understanding of the person and work of the Messiah? Some think so. But I am not so sure. Although it is true that Jesus wants them to understand who He is, I think that when Jesus says that what will happen in the raising of Lazarus is "so that you may believe," He is referring to something more than creedal certainty. It's not simply about coming to a correct theological assessment of Jesus' identity.

Where do we see this? In the interaction that Jesus has with those He meets in Bethany.

When reading about the resurrection of Lazarus, it is easy to get your attention fixed squarely on Lazarus; after all, he does appear to be a main (although silent!) character in this account. But he is not the only one who should get some of our attention. Although Lazarus' death is the "presenting problem" in this account, Lazarus himself is hardly a prominent actor in this story—he has only a "walk on" part toward the end. In particular, we need to pay attention to Martha's confession of faith in Jesus and her subsequent conversation with Jesus at the tomb.

MARTHA BELIEVES

As Jesus approaches Bethany, Martha (Lazarus' sister) receives word that He is in the vicinity. She goes out to meet Him. In her exchange with Jesus, she affirms a number of significant things. Specifically . . .

She affirms her confidence that Jesus can heal the sick.

She acknowledges with certainty that Jesus can ask God for anything and it will happen.

She confesses she believes that there will be a resurrection of the dead.

She declares she knows that Jesus Himself is the one with power to raise the dead.

She concurs with Jesus in asserting that those who believe in Him will never face death but will live forever.

She freely offers that she recognizes that Jesus is the promised Messiah, God's Deliverer and Redeemer.

She announces her certainty that Jesus is the Son of God who has come to earth.

She sounds like she has the right perspective. She believes the right things. She probably could articulate who Jesus is better than some who attend church these days. If this is her answer to the question, "Martha, what do you believe?" it is hard to fault her. She seems to have her thinking straight with regard to Jesus. She knows who He is. She would have easily passed the test for "sound doctrine" in most any church.[140]

But apparently that wasn't enough. It would seem Jesus was looking for something more. That becomes clear as we listen carefully to their exchanges.

LATER, AT THE TOMB

After arriving at the tomb, Jesus makes a simple request of Martha. "Please roll away the stone."

Martha replies in a reasonable way—let me paraphrase her words. "Well, I'd prefer to not do that. Lazarus has been dead for four days and, you know, in this climate and these conditions, he will really smell. Let's not."

Jesus answers her and says (and here I am *not* paraphrasing), "Did I not say to you, if you believe, you will see the glory of God?"[141]

Those words startle me. Jesus said, "*If* you believe . . ." To Martha. To the one who made all the right confessions. The one who declared what she believed about Jesus. The one whose doctrine seems so right. What Jesus is implying is that she *doesn't believe.*

What is He saying? Doesn't Jesus think she really is convinced that He is the Messiah? Is Jesus concerned that in the space of a few minutes she has gone from making clear and certain statements about Him to having serious doubts about who He is? Is

Jesus questioning how she could end up not knowing who He is—moments after she confidently affirmed that He was the Son of God?

It is hard for me to imagine that is what Jesus is implying. In His request, He isn't asking Martha to reaffirm some truth. He asked her to roll away the stone. And she hesitated; she resists; she is reluctant. Why?

Because she's not willing to trust His judgment. She is not relying on Him.

It's one thing to affirm all the right things about Jesus. It is another thing to really trust Him.

It's like that couple who have been going together for a long time. They've come to know one another (or at least know *about* one another) pretty well. She has come to the point where she thinks the world of him; she really thinks he is marriage material. Then one day, he says, "I really love you. Let's get married." And she hesitates. Typically, such hesitation arises for one of two reasons: either she isn't sure she wants to get married, or she isn't sure she trusts him enough to risk this great adventure of marriage.

When Martha hesitates in rolling away the stone as Jesus asked, it is unlikely that she resists because she doesn't want her brother alive again. ("Uh-oh! I just got a great deal on all of Lazarus' bedroom furniture. This is going to look really bad if he comes back to life. Maybe I can stall Jesus.")

It would seem the catch is in her willingness to trust Jesus in this particular way. She questions His plan. She doesn't completely trust Him.

This was hinted at in the earlier exchange. She had said to Jesus, "If only You had been here . . ." It's hard to fault her given the situation—her brother had died even though she had sent word to Jesus. I doubt I would have responded as well as she did. But even in these words there is something suggestive.

When she says, "If only You had been here then . . ." she is implying something about how she thought things *should have gone*. In so doing, she subtly questions Jesus' timing, Jesus' plans.

FACTS ABOUT JESUS ARE NOT ENOUGH

In our first study—about the miracle at the wedding feast of Cana—we explored the idea that Biblical faith is more than an affirmation of truths about Jesus. Biblical faith moves through the truths about Jesus to a place where we really trust Him, personally. We take Him at His word; we rely on Him implicitly. That is a significant component to Biblical faith. And that is what Martha was lacking.

Jesus says, "Did I not tell you *if you believe* . . ." She doesn't believe Him in the sense that she isn't trusting Him to do what is best, what is right, what is proper, what is acceptable. She questions whether *how* He wants to deal with her longing—the raising of her brother—is really the best way to go.

But if she only will trust Him, Jesus promises her she will see something of the glory of God. What an incredible thought. Trusting Jesus in what He wants to do will result in us seeing something of the glory of God.

This is in line with what Jesus told His disciples earlier. Before going to see Lazarus (and after declaring that Lazarus was, in fact, dead), Jesus had said, "I am glad for your sake that I was not there, so that you may believe." Jesus did not want them merely to come to a correct theological understanding of His Messiahship. He wanted them to trust Him with regard to His timing, His understanding, His will, His desires, His plan.

Why did Jesus wait as long as He did? Had he gone to Bethany in response to the servant's message, He would have arrived just about the time Lazarus died. He could still have raised Lazarus from the dead—if all He was looking to do was prove something about His power over death. But He was interested in more than that.

Jesus waited as long as He did so that when He arrived He could cultivate in those who were following Him a sense that even in this—something that seemed so out of place—He could be trusted. He was seeking to create an environment where real faith, real trust, real dependency on Him could grow.

MOVING THROUGH TRUTH TO PERSONAL TRUST

At the center of Martha's struggle with Jesus is the issue of whether she will personally trust Him with something as troubling and challenging and heart wrenching as her brother's death. Can she rest in Jesus' timing and understanding? Can she relinquish her tendency to want things on her terms, the way she thinks they would best be handled, in order to rely on Jesus and take Him at His word? Even when Jesus' words seem, on the surface, to be so unreasonable?

Even when Martha is so clear on who Jesus is, she stumbles over how He wants her to trust Him.

That is the struggle I repeatedly face in my journey with Jesus in life. I get brought to crisis points where I have to move through the truth I know about Jesus and come to find new ways of trusting Him.

In the midst of a troubled relationship, you will hear Him say, "I want you to forgive." And you will find a Martha-like response rising in your heart: "You want me to do what? You don't understand. Forgiveness won't work in this situation. That's unreasonable."

In dealing with family and co-workers, you may hear Him say, "You need to serve others the way I serve you." And you will hear echoes of Martha's words in your own ears. "Why would I serve them? They don't appreciate me. That can't be the right thing. That's unreasonable."

Jesus calls husbands to love their wives—even when the wives don't seem to reciprocate. Jesus asks wives to respect their husbands—in spite of things the husbands do that seem unloving. Jesus instructs His followers to pour out their lives in service to others—although we often question whether such an investment will have any tangible return.

In each of these situations—and others just like them—the issue will not be whether we can affirm the truth about who Jesus is, but whether we will abandon ourselves to Him and His counsel. His call to you may well sound as unreasonable as rolling the stone away from a four-day-old tomb. But what He really wants is for us to press forward in what we know about Him and actually trust Him.

Rely on Jesus intentionally. This will take more than the right answers on a systematic theology exam, because Jesus is interested in a relationship with you—and that relationship is built on really trusting Him.

REFLECTING ON THIS TRUTH

FOR PERSONAL REFLECTION:

1. Even when we know the truth about Jesus, we don't always rest in Him, depend on Him, trust Him. Particularly when we are facing those defining moments in life when fear or uncertainty grips us. Where do you find it hardest to move from thinking true things about Jesus to truly trusting Him personally? Think about how and when you hesitate to give into something you know He wants for you. As He shows you, apologize for settling for knowing truth about Him and not personally trusting Him.

2. Jesus told Martha that seeing God's glory on display was going to be anchored in her trusting Him, her truly believing Him. Isn't that what you want? Don't you want to see God's glory on display in your life, in your world? Don't settle for trying to manage your life's difficulties while utilizing some of Jesus' resources. Abandon yourself to Jesus, personally—no matter what the challenge or struggle. In that way you will grow to know Him better and you will better be able to see how God intends to put His glory on display.

FOR GROUP DISCUSSION:

1. Reading back over Martha's confession of what she believes to be true about Jesus, which of her affirmations could you readily make? How does your view of Jesus overlap with hers?

2. Using your sanctified imagination, reflect on what might have been going on in Martha's heart and mind when she hesitated in following Jesus' word to roll away the stone. What do you imagine was the disconnect between what she knew about Jesus and her reluctance to roll the stone away? When have you experienced that kind of disconnect in your journey with Jesus?

3. What is the impact of knowing that Jesus purposefully waited for days before going to the aid of Martha, Mary, and Lazarus? Seeing what Jesus intended in that apparent delay, how might you be better prepared for a growing faith in Him when things don't play out the way you think they should?

CHAPTER THIRTEEN

WANTING TO BE ALL IN

WHAT THOMAS GOT TO SEE

Then [Jesus] said to Thomas, "Reach here with your finger, and see My hands; and reach here your hand and put it into My side; and do not be unbelieving, but believing."

—John 20:27

HAVE YOU EVER NOTICED THAT sometimes the people you meet do not live up to (or down to) the reports you have heard about them?

Maybe it is someone well known. He has a reputation of being kind and gracious; at least that is the kind of role he plays in the movies. She is heralded as thoughtful and attentive; clearly she must be that way, because of how she writes. Then you meet him; you spend a little time with her. And you come away surprised. The reputation doesn't match up with the reality.

Sometimes the poor match-up turns out to be a good thing. The lead-up seems to suggest that he's actually gruff and arrogant and smug; but you end up finding him appropriately attentive and personable. Everything you've been told about her focuses on how superficial she is, concerned about her image; but you discover she is thoughtful and deep and compassionate.

It doesn't matter what gives rise to the disconnect between person and press. It might be the result of simple misperception; it could be the mismanagement of public appearances. Perhaps rumors started out of jealousy or even animosity. But there are those times when—for good or for bad—the person and the press do not correspond well.

I think that this issue of a disconnect can, at times, interfere with our reading Scripture well. The "press" that we have heard or learned about certain characters we meet in the Biblical text can set us up for reading their stories wrong. Embracing the reputation we've heard, we then pay only scant attention to what the text actually says, and we end up only confirming the preconceived idea we have of the person—whether good or bad.

THEY'RE JUST A BUNCH OF . . .

It's not uncommon to hear people say, "The Jews rejected Jesus." To my way of thinking, that's a "bad press" problem. It is true that a significant number of Jewish leaders (as well as Gentile leaders) did oppose Jesus and agitate for His death. But the rumor that "the Jews rejected Jesus" is hard to reconcile with the fact that all of Jesus' earliest followers were Jews and that the Christian church has its roots in the Jewish community in Jerusalem.

Sometimes Bible readers will talk about how the Pharisees "were a bunch of hypocrites." Now there are a number of passages that speak of the hypocrisy of the Pharisees.[142] But the Pharisees were not the only ones called out for hypocrisy.[143] Also, some Pharisees do appear to have had a genuine interest in Jesus.[144] One of Jesus' most well-known exchanges with an inquirer took place between Jesus and a Pharisee named Nicodemus, a man who seems sincere in his questions.[145]

When Jesus healed a blind man, as we read about in John 9, there was a "division among [the Pharisees]" (9:16). Some were convinced Jesus could not be from God, while others argued for the opposite view.[146]

All this is to say that the reputation of the Pharisees as simply being a band of religious hypocrites may well be an overstatement. And that "press problem" can lead us to misread and misunderstand portions of the Gospels where we see an exchange between Jesus and the Pharisees.[147]

We need to come to the Gospels holding our preconceptions loosely. We don't like to be wrongly perceived, to be subject to an unfair prejudice or bias. We want people to look and listen to us as individuals, and not just treat us based on whatever they might have heard. Realizing this, we should approach those we meet in the pages of the Scripture with a similar courtesy.

As we turn our attention to the next miracle, this principle will be important. Why? Because one of the key figures in this passage is Thomas, someone I think has inappropriately suffered some bad press. Working through this passage, perhaps we will discover why it is wrong to think of him as "doubting Thomas."

DOUBTING THOMAS' REPUTATION

Even among those who are not frequent Bible readers, the nickname of *Doubter* appears to be used readily in referring to Thomas, one of the Twelve. The impetus for this descriptor comes from John 20:24–27.

Earlier in John's Gospel, Jesus presented Himself alive, after the resurrection, to His disciples. But Thomas had not been there. When those who saw the risen Lord told Thomas about it, he said to them, "Unless I see in His hands the imprint of the nails, and put my finger into the place of the nails, and put my hand into His side, I will not believe" (John 20:25). We will look in more detail at this exchange and Jesus' appearance to the disciples again (including Thomas), but it will beneficial to look at what else we are told about Thomas—before this "doubting" moment.

Apart from where we find him listed in the company of the apostles appointed by Jesus,[148] Thomas is only mentioned a few times—all in the Gospel of John.

As John writes about the death and subsequent resurrection of Jesus' friend Lazarus, we get a glimpse into Thomas and his thinking. Shortly before making the trip to raise Lazarus from his tomb, Jesus found Himself in a confrontation with some Jews in Judea. That conflict rose to the level of threats, as Jesus' opponents picked up stones to stone Him (John 10:31). Although these enemies sought to seize Him, Jesus escaped and left the region (10:39–40). Needless to say, Judea was not a safe place for Jesus.

After explaining to His followers that Lazarus had died, Jesus told them they were going to head back to Judea so that He could raise Lazarus (John 11:7–15). It is at that moment we get another glimpse of Thomas.

> So Jesus then said to them plainly, "Lazarus is dead, and I am glad for your sakes that I was not there, so that you may believe; but let us go to him." Therefore Thomas, who is called Didymus, said to his fellow disciples, "Let us go, so that we may die with Him."
>
> —John 11:14–16

Some read Thomas' words as if he is a pessimistic depressive sort; the apostolic bands' equivalent to Eeyore in the Winnie the Pooh tales, who always sees things in the worst possible light.[149] But that is not the only way to understand Thomas' remark.

If Thomas had rightly perceived the threat presented by the hostile people back in Judea, and if Thomas had rightly recognized that Jesus' death was only precluded by His having left that area, realizing that Jesus intended to return to that very region would likely lead Thomas to the reasonable—rather than merely pessimistic—conclusion that Jesus was going to face His (possible) death. And Thomas was willing to sign up for that. This sounds like a man of courage and commitment. In this little snapshot, Thomas appears to be a man who wants to be "all in" with Jesus.[150]

As Jesus does approach His death, He spends some time with His closest friends celebrating the Passover (John 14–17). There, in what is referred to as the Upper Room, Jesus explains to these men what their lives will be like when He is no longer physically present with them. In the exchange, we again hear from Thomas.

> [Jesus said,] "Do not let your heart be troubled; believe in God, believe also in Me. In My Father's house are many dwelling places; if it were not so, I would have told you; for I go to prepare a place for you. If I go and prepare a place for you, I will come again and receive you to Myself, that where I am, there you may be also. And you know the way where I am going." Thomas said to Him, "Lord, we do not know where You are going, how do we know the way?" Jesus said to him, "I am the way, and the truth, and the life; no one comes to the Father but through Me."
>
> —John 14:1–6

There is much more in these few verses than we can unpack here, but we can take note of a few things regarding Thomas and his exchange with Jesus.

Jesus called His followers to believe in Him—to trust what He is telling them. And He explained that He was going to "prepare a place" for them. However else we might make sense of the place Jesus was going to prepare, it includes Jesus' expectation that His disciples will be with Him. This is what prompts Thomas' question.

"We do not know where You are going, how do we know the way?" Thomas' concern is clear. "We know You are going. We know You are saying we can't go with You now. We know You are saying we will be able to join You later. But seeing as we don't know where You are going, how are we going to get there?"

What does this show us about Thomas? Minimally, we see someone who desperately wants to be with Jesus where He is. Coupled with the earlier snapshot of Thomas, we begin to see something about this man. He really is all about being with Jesus. He doesn't want to be left behind, to be separated from Jesus. As mentioned earlier, Thomas appears to be a man who is all in when it comes to life with Jesus.

That should help inform our understanding of what happened later, after the resurrection, when Jesus appeared to His followers—and to Thomas.

THE CRITICAL ENCOUNTER

We can now turn our attention to the last snapshot of Thomas found in John—the one that gives rise to the nickname, "Doubter."

> But Thomas, one of the twelve, called Didymus, was not with them when Jesus came. So the other disciples were saying to him, "We have seen the Lord!" But he said to them, "Unless I see in His hands the imprint of the nails, and put my finger into the place of the nails, and put my hand into His side, I will not believe."
>
> After eight days His disciples were again[151] inside, and Thomas with them. Jesus came, the doors having been shut, and stood in their midst and said, "Peace be with you." Then He said to Thomas, "Reach here with your finger, and see My hands; and reach here your hand and put it into My side; and do not be unbelieving, but believing." Thomas answered and said to Him, "My Lord and my God!" Jesus said to him, "Because you have seen

> Me, have you believed? Blessed are they who did not see, and yet believed."
>
> —John 20:24–29

Although sometimes not spoken of as a miracle, this appearance of Jesus certainly qualifies. Jesus physically showed up in the presence of His disciples while they were inside a locked room.[152] To make sense of this miracle and Jesus' exchange with Thomas, we need to be clear about the situation.

Jesus had already had one meeting with the rest of the apostles. He had spoken with them, confirming not only His resurrection but also their commission. There is no explanation for Thomas' absence; it seems relatively fruitless to speculate. He wasn't there, but when he did meet up with the rest after a short while, they sought to convince him of what they had seen.

"The other disciples were saying to him." This means they kept on trying to help Thomas understand; John's language indicates that it was more than a "once and done" sharing with Thomas. It is their persistence that prompts Thomas' statement: "Unless I see in His hands the imprint of the nails, and put my finger into the place of the nails, and put my hand into His side, I will not believe."

Now Jesus does, in presenting Himself to Thomas, say, "Do not be unbelieving, but believing." But what is Jesus calling for? What is it that Thomas is struggling with? Why does Thomas seem to place conditions on his believing?

How are we to understand Thomas' words? Here the bad press about Thomas might influence us. If we come into this account convinced that Thomas was just a doubter, then we can hear his words simply as confirming our preassessment. But what if we come into this passage with our thinking about Thomas shaped by what we've previously seen—that he seems to be a courageous, honest follower who gives every indication of being sold out for Jesus?

Thomas wants to have personal confirmation—"I want to see; I want to touch . . . only then will I believe." And he wants this in the face of the assertions of the other disciples.

What do we know of them? Well, up to this moment of Thomas' exchange with them, they have not been a group of men that stirs much confidence.

These disciples were the ones Jesus had said would abandon Him.[153] Thomas had been there when Jesus told them that one of their group would betray Him and that even Peter, the most vocal of the band, would deny knowing Jesus.[154] When Jesus was praying in the garden, before being handed over to the authorities, Thomas knew that these disciples had not even been able to continue with Jesus in His agony.[155] Other than with the possible exception of John, none of them were apparently present at the crucifixion. This isn't to make Thomas out to be better than the others, but to simply raise the question of the reliability of these men. It would seem that Thomas had some reasonable grounds for wondering about their credibility.

WHAT WOULD YOU WANT?

Drawing together the strands of thought that we have in our hands, how might we understand Thomas' exchange with the others? Let me fill in between the lines, trying to capture what might be the essence of what is being said.

The others, "We have seen the Lord!"

Thomas, "*You* have seen Him? Can I really take your word for that? You don't have a very good recent track record."

The others, "We really have seen Him!"

Thomas, "If He really is alive, I will be all in . . . and you? I am not so sure."

The others, "We have, we have seen Him alive."

Thomas, "For me to believe *you,* for me to be all in, I think I need to see Him for myself. Not an apparition, not a delusion. I need to know for sure, because I am willing to give my life for Him if He really is alive."

I would not insist that this is the only way to understand what Thomas said, but I think this is more consistent with the overall picture we have of Thomas. And I think it rings true when Thomas does come face to face with the risen Jesus.

> After eight days His disciples were again inside, and Thomas with them. Jesus came, the doors having been shut, and stood in their midst and said, "Peace be with you." Then He said to Thomas, "Reach here with your finger, and see My hands; and reach here your hand and put it into My side; and do not be unbelieving, but believing." Thomas answered and said to Him, "My Lord and my God!"
>
> —John 20:26–29

When Jesus did appear and invited Thomas to reach out and touch the marks on His body, Thomas didn't do that. Thomas' only response was to proclaim, "My Lord and my God." Apparently he didn't need the actual touch; he only wanted the absolute assurance. And Thomas' declaration exceeds that of any of the other disciples when they first saw the resurrection Jesus. It would seem that, being assured that Jesus was really alive, Thomas was indeed all in!

DOUBTS ABOUT THAT DOUBT

But Jesus did call Thomas to "not be unbelieving, but believing." Isn't there some doubt issue there? Some careful attention to the language is essential.

The "unbelieving" word is only found here in John's Gospel. But there are two other passages from the other Gospels that might be of help.

> While they were telling these things, [Jesus] Himself stood in their midst and said to them, "Peace be to you." But they were startled and frightened and thought that they were seeing a spirit. And He said to them, "Why are you troubled, and why do doubts arise in your hearts? See My hands and My feet, that it is I Myself; touch Me and see, for a spirit does not have flesh and bones as you see that I have." And when He had said this, He showed them His hands and His feet. While they still could not believe it because of their joy and amazement . . .
>
> —Luke 24:36–41

This appears to be the pre-Thomas resurrection encounter. There are a number of essential elements to note. First, these disciples were, themselves, reluctant to believe—even with Jesus standing in their midst! They were wrestling with doubts. Jesus offered them His hands and feet to assure them. (This sounds a lot like what Thomas wanted.) And "they still could not believe it because of their joy and amazement." This suggests that these other disciples had at least as great a struggle in believing as did Thomas. So his is not a unique doubting, but the others don't get the "doubting" label as did Thomas.[156]

Another place that helps us in understanding Thomas comes in an encounter Jesus had with a man whose son was oppressed by a demonic spirit. After the disciples could not help the man and his boy, the father approached Jesus. The father pled with Jesus.

> "But if You can do anything, take pity on us and help us!" And Jesus said to him, "'If You can?' All things are possible to him who believes." Immediately the boy's father cried out and said, "I do believe; help my unbelief."
>
> —Mark 9:22–24

It would seem, from the father's language, that he does want to trust Jesus, to believe Him for the help he needs. But the man also feels some unbelief. He wants to be entirely abandoned to Jesus in this moment of need, but he's struggling to get there. This suggests that the struggle to get to the place of entire abandonment in faith is not unique to Thomas.

Even the call to be believing that Jesus extended to Thomas needs careful thought. As we saw in the chapter on the raising of Lazarus,[157] in John's Gospel the idea of *believing* is more than just a matter of affirming Jesus' identity or agreeing with certain facts. There is a real sense that biblical *belief* or *faith*[158] includes a significant element of abandonment and dependence. Knowing about someone, to *believe* in him is the growing dependence upon, reliance on, trust in, and abandonment to that someone.

For Thomas, the problem may not have been a matter of incredulity about the possibility of the resurrection, but a desire to entirely abandon himself to Jesus *if it were the case that Jesus was really alive.* Because of the recent track record of the other disciples, Thomas could well have refrained from that kind of abandonment until he could be certain that the Jesus to whom he wanted to give Himself was, in truth, risen. Jesus' call to Thomas was then the invitation to be as all in as he truly wanted to be. "Don't be unbelieving (hesitant to abandon yourself to Me), but be believing (Give in completely, Thomas)."

When we watch Thomas' encounter with Jesus play out, it is clear that Thomas not only got what he longed for but that he really did see Jesus for who He was and abandoned himself to Jesus. This is captured in his short but profound confession, "My Lord and my God." Those are not words to be taken lightly. That is a massive declaration that can only come if it is backed up with massive abandonment.

WHAT WAS NEEDED

So, why this miracle? Why does Jesus present Himself alive to Thomas? He doesn't do this for everyone. Was Thomas a test case? Did he get some kind of special dispensation from Jesus? Would you not like to have the same experience Thomas did? Should we expect the same?

We can say for certain that Jesus did this for Thomas. What we can't say for certain is why this happened for him and why the same doesn't happen for us.

After appearing to Thomas, Jesus did explain: "Because you have seen Me, have you believed? Blessed are they who did not see, and yet believed." From this, some conclude that Thomas' experience was not only unique, but that others should not expect anything similar. But this cannot mean that Jesus is unwilling to provide evidence for belief to His disciples.

Jesus seemed quite intent to offer such evidence prior to His ascension. We've already noted (as recorded in Luke 24:36–11) that Jesus invited the other disciples to examine Him closely so as to be assured He was indeed risen from the dead. Luke also noted that Jesus "presented Himself alive [to His disciples] after His suffering, by many convincing proofs, appearing to them over a period of forty days" (Acts 1:3). In his letter to the Corinthians, Paul explained that Jesus had presented Himself alive to as many as five hundred at one time (1 Corinthians 15:6).

Jesus can and did present Himself alive to many. He did this because He wanted to; He chose to. He didn't have to do these things; He didn't have to reveal Himself the way He did to Thomas. But He did. And we need to think about what this might mean . . . and what it tells us about Jesus.

Looking back over the exchange between Jesus and Thomas, the intended outcome is clear. Jesus wanted Thomas to be believing. Jesus' desire was that there would be nothing that would keep

Thomas from being the "all in" man that Jesus had seen Thomas to be in their three-and-a-half years together. I would suggest that Jesus did what He did for Thomas because Jesus knew that would be needed to bring Thomas to that point.

Thomas wanted to follow Jesus. He was desperate to be with Jesus, wherever Jesus was. Even if it might mean dying with Him. Thomas didn't want to be apart from Jesus. When Jesus spoke of leaving, Thomas was the one who asked for directions so he could go to join up with Him. Could it be that this miracle was Jesus' gracious gift to Thomas so that there would be nothing in the way of Thomas getting what he wanted, which was to fully follow Jesus?

Early in Jesus' ministry, some of His listeners were raising questions about whether what Jesus was saying and doing was really the will of God. Jesus responded with a provocative assertion: "If anyone is willing to do [God's] will, he will know of the teaching, whether it is of God" (John 7:17).

What is so intriguing about this is that Jesus is insisting that a willingness to do the will of God may precede an understanding of what the will of God is. The heart inclination—a desire to be all in—may well be needed before knowing the teaching.

As I continue my journey with Jesus, I find that I often have those two pieces reversed. I want to know the will of God before I abandon myself to do the will of God. I would like to have the option of assessing whether what God wants for me is what I would like to do or to be. I want the knowing of His will before I incline my will to the doing.

I wrestle with decisions, not because I am wholly lacking clarity about the options, but because I am genuinely ambiguous about whether I want to do the will of God (if it turns out to be my "B" choice rather than my "A" choice). And, so often, when my heart settles into an attitude of "wherever you take me, Lord, that is where I want to go," I find clarity and direction. I know . . . after the willing.

I think Thomas had the pieces right. He was inclined to do all that Jesus wanted for him; he wanted to be with Jesus, participating with Him, in all that He was doing. Given that, all that was needed was for Thomas to be sure what it was that Jesus wanted—and at that moment in time it included assurance that Jesus was alive (and that such reports were not merely the less-than-certain testimony of the somewhat unreliable disciples).

It would be wrong to conclude that everyone who sincerely longs to follow Jesus will have an experience identical to the one Thomas had with Jesus. But it would be right to think that Jesus, the good shepherd, will give whatever is necessary to His sheep who long to follow Him wherever He might take them.

Jesus said, "I am the good shepherd; the good shepherd lays down His life for the sheep. . . . I am the good shepherd, I know My own and My own know Me. . . My sheep hear My voice, and I know them, and they follow Me; and I give eternal life to them." (John 10:11, 14, 27–28)

REFLECTING ON THIS TRUTH

FOR PERSONAL REFLECTION:

1. It's easy to be hard on Thomas, concluding that we would never be as doubting as he was. But as you look carefully at all we are told about him, a different picture emerges. In what ways do you think you are like Thomas? In what ways do you think you are different from him?

2. Jesus was willing to present Himself alive to the other disciples (when Thomas wasn't there). He offered convincing proofs that He was alive to others (Acts 1:3). In what ways is Jesus' exchange with Thomas similar to those other accounts? How does what Jesus did for Thomas differ from those other situations?

3. When Thomas is convinced that Jesus is alive, he freely proclaims, "My Lord and My God." What do you think that confession meant for him? What would you need from Jesus in order to be able to declare the same thing . . . and live out the essence of that declaration? Talk to Jesus about what keeps you back from living all in the way Thomas did.

FOR GROUP DISCUSSION:

1. What preconceived ideas have you had about Thomas? What has given rise to these ideas? Do you think those preconceived ideas are warranted? Why or why not?

2. Given the experiences Thomas had with the other disciples, do you think he was justified in questioning whether he could believe their witness about Jesus being alive? What do you think you would have done had you found yourself in Thomas' situation?

3. Jesus doesn't promise to grant to every believer the same experience He granted Thomas. But He did provide Thomas what he needed to go all in with Jesus. Do you think you are willing to be all in the way Thomas appeared to be?

CHAPTER FOURTEEN

EPILOGUE

WHERE DO HIS MIRACLES TAKE YOU?

But grow in the grace and knowledge of our Lord and Savior Jesus Christ. To Him be the glory, both now and to the day of eternity. Amen.

—2 Peter 3:18

I REMEMBER THE FIRST FEW years of struggling to get grass to grow in my backyard. Although my desire was to have a nice green yard that could be enjoyed by children and pets, it just wasn't happening. Throughout the season, I did what I thought was right. But the grass would brown out during the summer and barely hang on during the cool months.

It was only after some extended conversations with a friend who had studied landscape management that I came to realize that my efforts, though well intentioned, were misguided. I didn't know what my grass needed in order to develop well.

I now have a nice backyard. It hasn't been terribly difficult—once I knew what was necessary. Grass naturally grows. I haven't done anything magical; I only did what grass needs.

Grass, given what it needs—the right climate and fertilizer and sufficient water—does grow.

This is true about all living things. When living things are provided what is needed for life, they grow. It's true about natural living things; it is also true about spiritual living things.

In his second letter, the apostle Peter wrote that Christians should "grow in the grace and knowledge of our Lord and Savior Jesus Christ" (2 Peter 3:18). We could read Peter's words as if he is saying that Christians will grow, do grow, as they walk with the Lord. In one sense, there is truth in that.

The life with Jesus we are enjoying is a work of grace. And, having begun that work in us, our kind and wise Lord and Savior will continue to work in us, bringing us to His intended end (Philippians 1:6). But Peter's language is more than an observation about how life does work; he is issuing a call, presenting a charge to every believer.

We are called to grow. This is an invitation to give ourselves to growing "in the grace and knowledge of our Lord and Savior Jesus Christ." This is not a call to passive but certain hope that we will grow, but a purposeful and intentional pursuit of what makes for growth.

Peter points to two areas for growth. Growth in the grace that is found in and through Jesus Christ. Growth in the knowledge of our Lord and Savior Jesus.

WHAT ABOUT YOU?

Over the past few years, I have repeatedly asked fellow Christ-followers if they sense or feel their own growth. "Are you experiencing grace in a richer and fuller and deeper way than you did last year? Have you grown in the grace that is ours through Jesus? Do you know more about Jesus and all He is for you and all He has done for you than you did six months ago? Have you grown to know Jesus better?" Sadly, many answer saying they are not aware of any real growth. It isn't that they don't know Jesus; it isn't that they are not standing in grace. It's just that they are not aware of any real growth.

Now it is possible that they are growing—but just not aware of it. As my son was growing during his middle school years, he was often concerned that nothing was happening! At that time being one of the shorter boys in his grade, the feeling that he was not getting any taller troubled him. Like many parents, we had consistently marked his growth on a wall in a corner of the house. I could take him there and show him. "See, you are a quarter of an inch taller than you were just a few months ago. You are growing!"

Sometimes it is like that in the Christian life. Because of God's goodness, we are growing. We might not be aware of it, we may not feel or sense any growth, but we could still be growing. But that is not always the case.

The author of the letter to the Hebrews, writing to Christians, comments about his readers that "by this time you ought to be teachers." But their apparent lack of growth has left them with a "need again for someone to teach you the elementary principles of the oracle of God" (Hebrews 5:12). In other words, they should have been growing, they could have been growing, but apparently they had not grown.

This thought brings us back to Peter's call. Grow! Grow to understand and live in grace better. Grow to know and relate to Jesus better. And that is where I hope this journey through some of the miracles of Jesus has led you—to growth.

As we have walked through a dozen of Jesus' miracles, recorded for us in the Gospels, have you discovered anything new about how He extends grace? Have you caught a glimpse of some yet untasted experience of Jesus' kindness and wisdom and goodness? What would it be like to embrace that offer of grace, pictured in these miracles? How could you step more fully into "the grace of our Lord and Savior Jesus Christ"?

As we explored what Jesus did and how He ministered, as pictured for us in the Gospels, have you seen anything new about Him? Have your heart and your imagination been stirred with some unexpected quality or character trait not yet seen in Him? How would your relationship with Him grow and change if you took what you have learned and integrated those truths into the way you relate to Him? How could you be thoughtful about your growth "in the knowledge of our Lord and Savior Jesus Christ"?

THE JOURNEY CONTINUES

1. How might you keep the growing going? What could help you continue to lean into what Jesus has been doing in you through this study?

2. Read Scripture. It isn't that other books (like this one!) aren't of help. But don't lose sight of what is the essential nutrient for

good spiritual growth—the Word of God.[159] Hopefully, the expositions found in this study modeled that. Hopefully, these chapters weren't an end in themselves, but they served to nudge you to read passages from the Gospels, reflect well on what you read, and respond to the truth that is there, in the Word of God.

3. Think well.[160] At times, it is our perception that we "already know that" when we come to a portion of Scripture that keeps us from encountering Jesus in fresh and real ways. Hopefully, the expositions found in this study modeled that. Hopefully, these discussions didn't merely tell you what to think, but encouraged you to engage mind and heart and think freshly and deeply about God's revelation to us.

4. Ask passionately. The Spirit who inspired the Word is also the Spirit who guides us in our study.[161] Although it would be wrong to assume we could grow in the grace and knowledge of our Lord and Savior Jesus Christ without applying ourselves to the call to read and know Scripture, it would also be wrong to assume that a mere intellectual endeavor will result in the fruitfulness we long for. Invite the Spirit to open the eyes of your soul to see all He has in store for you in Scripture.

5. Discuss honestly. Not one of us has a corner on the truth. We all have blind spots. There are things in a passage that we quickly and unintentionally read right over, but that are so very apparent to others. Welcome others into honest dialogue about what you are reading, what you are seeing, and how you are growing to understand more and more about grace and about Jesus.[162]

APPENDIX ONE

DOES JESUS EVER PULL OUT HIS "GOD CARD"?

You know of Jesus of Nazareth, how God anointed Him with the Holy Spirit and with power, and how He went about doing good and healing all who were oppressed by the devil, for God was with Him.

—Acts 10:38

THROUGHOUT THIS BOOK, WE HAVE looked at Jesus' miracles as if His proving His divinity was not His primary concern. In doing miracles, Jesus is not pulling out His "God card."

Some authors do adopt a "God card" approach to Jesus' miracles in order to defend the doctrine of Jesus' divinity.[163] The desire to affirm Jesus' divinity is right. However, as has been noted, the argument that Jesus' miracles prove His divinity may be theologically inconsistent.[164] To argue against a "God card" perspective does not mean there should be any question of Jesus' divinity—He is the second person of the Godhead incarnate. The Scriptures make this clear.[165] But that He performed signs and wonders is not, in and of itself, proof that He is God.

In the Gospels, when Jesus does something miraculous, the eyewitnesses of those wonders do not typically draw the conclusion that Jesus is therefore divine.

WHAT DID THEY UNDERSTAND?

When Jesus taught in the synagogue and subsequently delivered a man from an oppressive evil spirit (Mark 1:21–28), all those who saw this moment were amazed. However, the issue raised by what they saw was about the authority with which Jesus did what He did. Apparently no one felt that His display of authority automatically led to the idea that Jesus was making a divine claim.

When Jesus spoke a word of healing and forgiveness to the paralyzed man who had been lowered through the roof (Mark 3:1–6), the scribes did question the appropriateness of Jesus' extending forgiveness. But as we saw in exploring that passage, it might not have been that the scribes understood Jesus' offer of forgiveness as an explicit divine claim.[166] All who were present at the healing and heard the offer of forgiveness were amazed; no one, however, left the house insisting that Jesus must, therefore, be God.

In the extended account of Jesus' healing of a blind man (John 9:1–38), we hear the thinking of many different people regarding what Jesus had done and what it meant. But apparently no one wrestled with whether Jesus' miraculous healing should lead to the conclusion that He was divine. Even the man's response in faith—stating that Jesus was "the Son of Man" (John 9:38)—is not necessary proof that the man had concluded that Jesus was God come in the flesh.[167]

After an extensive and widespread ministry of miracle-working and healing and deliverance, when Jesus asked His friends who people thought He was, they explained that the people had a variety of conclusions—John the Baptist resurrected, Elijah, one of the prophets of the Old Testament (Matthew 15:13–14). Hearing such assessments, Jesus did not throw up His hands in exasperation and say, "You mean that the people don't see? They don't understand? They still don't recognize that I am God come in the flesh?"

It would be improper, though, to conclude that Jesus' miracles were entirely disconnected from His divine nature or His divine claims. But the connection—for there is one—needs to be well thought out.

When a religious leader named Nicodemus visited Jesus by night, he affirmed that Jesus could not do the things He had been doing if God were not "with him" (John 3:2). Peter, in speaking to a God-fearing Gentile named Cornelius, explained that Jesus had been anointed by God and went around "doing good" through God's power (Acts 10:38). Such statements point out that Jesus' miracles and signs did have some attesting value—they indicated that God was supporting Jesus. Jesus had the approval of God.

It is in seeing this idea of God's approval through the signs that we can find some evidential support for Jesus' divinity in His miracles.

AND HE SAID . . .

Jesus made claims about Himself that would have been entirely inappropriate for any mere human—even a prophet or priest—to make. He said things that came with a "divine ring" to them.

God makes it clear, in any number of passages in the Old Testament, that faith—ultimate trust—is to be placed in Him alone.

> "Turn to Me and be saved, all the ends of the earth; for I am God, and there is no other."
>
> —Isaiah 45:22

> Thus says the LORD, "Cursed is the man who trusts in mankind and makes flesh his strength, and whose heart turns away from the LORD. . . . Blessed is the man who trusts in the LORD and whose trust is the LORD."
>
> —Jeremiah 17:5, 7

Seeing how God speaks of Himself as the only proper object of faith, Jesus' statement that all men should put faith in Him, should trust Him, is a divine claim. Jesus said things like:

> "Therefore I said to you that you will die in your sins; for unless you believe that I am He, you will die in your sins."
>
> —John 8:24

> "Do not let your heart be troubled; believe in God, believe also in Me."
>
> —John 14:1

When Jesus speaks about Scripture—God's Word—the way He speaks come with a divine claim as well. Jesus said things like:

> "You search the Scriptures because you think that in them you have eternal life; it is these that testify about Me; and you are unwilling to come to Me so that you may have life."
>
> —John 5:39–40

> "Heaven and earth will pass away, but My words will not pass away."
>
> —Mark 13:31

On a number of occasions when Jesus is in conflict with Jewish leaders, what He says about Himself drives them to raise serious questions about how He thinks about Himself. His opponents think He is making some kind of divine claim, and Jesus does not deny it.

> For this reason the Jews were persecuting Jesus, because He was doing these things on the Sabbath. But He answered them, "My Father is working until now, and I Myself am working." For this reason therefore the Jews were seeking all the more to kill Him, because He not only was breaking the Sabbath, but also was calling God His own Father, making Himself equal with God.
>
> Therefore Jesus answered and was saying to them, "Truly, truly, I say to you, the Son can do nothing of Himself,

> unless it is something He sees the Father doing; for whatever the Father does, these things the Son also does in like manner. For the Father loves the Son, and shows Him all things that He Himself is doing; and the Father will show Him greater works than these, so that you will marvel. For just as the Father raises the dead and gives them life, even so the Son also gives life to whom He wishes. For not even the Father judges anyone, but He has given all judgment to the Son, so that all will honor the Son even as they honor the Father. He who does not honor the Son does not honor the Father who sent Him."
>
> —John 5:16–23

These Jews believed Jesus was asserting a privileged standing with God in the way He spoke about His relationship with the Father—they understood it as a claiming to be like God, to be divine. In responding, Jesus did not deny the claim. His assertion of His equality with the Father in a variety of ways was nothing short of a claim to share God's nature.

A bit later in John's Gospel we encounter another similar exchange:

> [Jesus said,] "I and the Father are one."
>
> The Jews picked up stones again to stone Him. Jesus answered them, "I showed you many good works from the Father; for which of them are you stoning Me?" The Jews answered Him, "For a good work we do not stone You, but for blasphemy; and because You, being a man, make

> Yourself out to be God." Jesus answered them . . . "If I do not do the works of My Father, do not believe Me; but if I do them, though you do not believe Me, believe the works, so that you may know and understand that the Father is in Me, and I in the Father." Therefore they were seeking again to seize Him, and He eluded their grasp.
>
> —John 10:30–39

Again we see Jews who had been listening to Jesus wrestle with the question of whether He was making a unique self-identification with God. Jesus not only doesn't deny it, but offers reason for them to agree with His self-identification.

Given such claims, what is the relationship between Jesus' self-identification, His miracles, and His pulling out His "God card"?

CAN I GET A WITNESS?

One way forward in our thinking comes by looking to an Old Testament prophet and the miracles he performed. In the days of Elijah, the king of Israel was at odds with the God of Israel. Because of that, the king did not particularly appreciate Elijah. Wanting to have a meeting with the prophet, King Ahaziah sent soldiers to bring Elijah to him. And something remarkable happened.

> Then the king sent to [Elijah] a captain of fifty with his fifty. And [the captain] went up to him, and behold, he was sitting on the top of the hill. And he said to him, "O man of God, the king says, 'Come down.'" Elijah replied to the captain of fifty, "If I am a man of God, let fire

> come down from heaven and consume you and your fifty." Then fire came down from heaven and consumed him and his fifty. So [Ahaziah] again sent to [Elijah] another captain of fifty with his fifty. And he said to him, "O man of God, thus says the king, 'Come down quickly.'" Elijah replied to them, "If I am a man of God, let fire come down from heaven and consume you and your fifty." Then the fire of God came down from heaven and consumed him and his fifty.
>
> —2 Kings 1:9–12

Here we see a miracle—fire falls from heaven at Elijah's word. But it would be wrong to assert that such command over nature must mean that Elijah is divine. When we listen to Elijah's self-identification, we hear his claim to be a "man of God"—he is a man, but one who is uniquely living in relationship with God. What does the miracle of the fire from heaven prove? That God is backing up Elijah's self-claim.

The miracle is God's way of affirming that what Elijah is saying about himself and his relationship with God is true. God would not have answered by fire—providing a "witness" to the rightness of Elijah's claim—if it wasn't true.

The same kind of confirmation through a miraculous sign is seen in another snapshot from Elijah's life. The episode is recorded for us in 1 Kings 18.

> The nation has turned from the true God and has begun worshipping false gods and idols. Under God's direction, Elijah presents a challenge. The false prophets of

> Ba'al (the chief idol to whom the nation had turned) and Elijah were to have a showdown. Two altars and two sacrifices would be prepared. The prophets of Ba'al were to cry out to their god, and Elijah would call out to the God of Israel. And, the God who answered by fire would be seen to be the true God. We pick up the account as Elijah begins preparing to call out to God.
>
> At the time of the offering of the evening sacrifice, Elijah the prophet came near and said, "O LORD, the God of Abraham, Isaac and Israel, today let it be known that You are God in Israel and that I am Your servant and I have done all these things at Your word. Answer me, O LORD, answer me, that this people may know that You, O LORD, are God, and that You have turned their heart back again." Then the afire of the LORD fell and consumed the burnt offering and the wood and the stones and the dust, and licked up the water that was in the trench. When all the people saw it, they fell on their faces; and they said, "The LORD, He is God; the LORD, He is God."
>
> —1 Kings 18:36–39

By answering by fire—providing a miraculous display—God affirmed the truthfulness of Elijah's claim—that he was God's servant and had done what he did according to God's instructions. The miracle attested to God's affirmation of Elijah's claim.

Understanding this, when we look back to Jesus' claims and the miracles He performed we can rightly see evidential value to

His miracles. The miracles do affirm and underscore the truth of Jesus' claims to be God. God would not have supported and confirmed Jesus' claims with incredible displays of power if His claims were misleading or untruthful or idolatrous.

In making this argument, there is no intention to diminish the deity of Jesus; He is God come in the flesh. It is in looking at His miracles and what He intends to communicate through them that the question of their proof value is raised. To say that Jesus' miracles do not, in themselves, prove He is divine is not to argue that He is merely a man; only to say that we must look at Jesus' life as a whole (and not just at the miraculous signs) for the full argument for His divinity.

JESUS AND THE SPIRIT

It is worth noting that the Gospels do offer some explanation for the power that is at work in and through Jesus. Although often ignored, these explanations tend to confirm the approach taken in this book toward understanding His miracles.

As Jesus began His ministry, Luke wrote that He came into Galilee "in the power of the Spirit" (Luke 4:14). Jesus did not begin His public ministry in the power of His own divine life, but in the power the Spirit provided.[168]

When confronted about His ministry of deliverance by some Jewish leaders, Jesus declared that He "cast out demons by the Spirit of God" (Matthew 12:28). Jesus did not assert that He dealt with demonic problems on the basis of His own divine nature.

In the Upper Room as He was talking with His closest friends about how they were going to carry on after His physical departure from the planet, Jesus told about His relationship with the Father and their coming relationship with Him. He told them that what they had witnessed in Him was not, fundamentally, His divine works; He insisted "the Father abiding in Me does His works" (John 14:10). He is saying that the miraculous things they had witnessed were the works of His Father. And then He went on to explain that the one who "believes in Me, the works I do, he will do also" (14:12). In the context of the Upper Room (and the broader context of John), *works* refers to Jesus' miracles. As Jesus goes on to explain to His followers, those who believe will do the same works He did (through the power of the Spirit who they would receive).

If Jesus did the miracles He did in the power of His own divine nature—if they were proofs that He was divine—it would be both unreasonable and impossible for Him to suggest that His followers could do the same. But if Jesus' ministry was carried out in the power of the Spirit then His disciples could do the same. And they did.

The twelve did the same kinds of things Jesus Himself did.[169] The seventy did the same kinds of things that Jesus Himself did.[170] In the book of Acts, we read about people like Stephen and Philip doing things similar to what Jesus Himself did.[171] The miracles they did were not proof they were divine—but they were attestations given by God that He was confirming the message they brought and that they were empowered by the same Spirit who empowered Jesus.

Where does this leave us? Does Jesus ever pull out His "God card"?

We could summarize the answer to this question in a simple way:

Jesus is God, the divine Second Person of the Trinity incarnate;

Jesus performed miracles;

Jesus' miracles affirmed the message He brought and what He had to say about Himself thus substantiating His divine claims;

Jesus' miracles tell us more about Him than simply proving His divine nature.

APPENDIX TWO

LEARNING TO READ GOSPEL NARRATIVES

And there are also many other things which Jesus did, which if they were written in detail, I suppose that even the world itself would not contain the books that would be written.

—John 21:25

FOR DECADES, I HAVE HAD the joy of both teaching the Bible and helping others learn to read and understand the Bible. One of the essential components to both good teaching and proper understanding of Scripture is knowing how to make sense of Biblical narratives—seeing as a large percentage of the Bible is narrative.

A narrative is a story—but not a fictional story like the novels we read or the movies we watch. Biblical narratives are true stories, presenting truth-in-life. Quite typically, the Bible stories we have come to know and love are narratives. Old Testaments accounts telling us about Abraham and Jacob, David and Solomon, or heroes like Samson or Gideon are all narratives. Turning to the New Testaments, the Gospels and Acts are, for the most part, narratives as well.

The Gospel narratives are a record of how Jesus stepped into our world in the Incarnation. They tell us what He taught and what He did. They give us snapshots of His interactions with people just like us and, in so doing, help us grasp what He is like and what it might mean for us to have life with Him.

READ "THERE"

One of the best ways to understand a narrative is to "enter" the story. This is not an invitation to assume that you are living the life of the characters in the narrative; we don't pretend we are that person we see in the narrative. However, since the Gospel narratives reveal to us how Jesus interacted with people and how He revealed Himself to them in the events recorded, to "be there" helps us make sense of what God is revealing. That is why, as we explore the miracle accounts, we need to think about how those in the story were living in the moment.

For example, if we are reading Mark 3:1–6 and the account of Jesus' ministering to the man with the withered hand, we should seek to "live there," in the narrative. What would the man be feeling? Thinking? What about those watching what was happening? What would it have been like to be in that moment? And we need to pay close attention to what Jesus did and how He is revealing Himself—He is the main character in any Gospel narrative.

When seeking to understand a narrative, there are a few interpretive approaches it would be best to resist.

AVOID READING NARRATIVES AS "LIFE PRINCIPLES"

When we adopt this approach, we tend to read the narrative as if it is directive. We conclude, fundamentally, that what happened to the person we meet in the narrative is a call to us to do the same thing. We then translate the events into an instruction set.

One common example of this life principle approach arises when we read about Jesus' early post-Sabbath morning activity.

> In the early morning, while it was still dark, Jesus got up, left the house, and went away to a secluded place, and was praying there.
>
> —Mark 1:35

Perhaps you've heard someone explain that this text is teaching the following:

> Jesus got up early to have a "morning quiet time."
>
> If Jesus needed to do this, we should do this as well.
>
> You should have a regular morning quite time, meeting with God.

Now I am not opposed to having regular time with God. I am not even opposed to taking some of that time early in the morning—I am a morning person so that works for me. But I do not think this small narrative piece is intended to teach either that Jesus had regular morning quiet times or that we are supposed to do the same.

If that were indeed the principle to be learned from this passage, then shouldn't we do our morning quiet time the way Jesus did? That is . . .

Set aside time while it is still dark,

Leave our house,

Go to a secluded place, and

Spend the entire time praying.

I don't think getting up after the sun is up, putting on my robe, getting a cup of coffee, finding a comfy chair, and reading a good devotional book before asking the Lord to guide me through the day looks even remotely like what Jesus did. And the kicker is that although in this passage we find Jesus rising early to pray, there are other passages that tell us how Jesus prayed late into the night or all through the night.[172] I don't ever hear anyone insisting, from those narrative passages, that the only way to have a regular "quiet time" is to spend whole nights in prayer.

This isn't to say that as we read a Gospel narrative and watch Jesus interact with people that we can't learn something about how we could or should respond to Him. As is clear from the discussions of the various miracles, there are practical things to be learned from a narrative about how we can enjoy life with Jesus. But learning from the story is different from reducing the story to an instructional set or some "life principle" to put into practice.

AVOID READING NARRATIVES AS ALLEGORIES

A variation of the life principle approach to reading narratives is to read the narrative as if it were an allegory. An allegory is a tale where there is a one-to-one kind of correspondence between elements of the tale and real life outside the story. Paul Bunyan's *Pilgrim's Progress,* for example, is a popular and widely read allegorical story that symbolizes the Christian life.

When we adopt this approach, we tend to minimize what is happening in the narrative and risk making too much of a "hidden" pattern of correspondence between the narrative elements and our own life.

As touched on in the chapter dealing with the miracle at the wedding feast in Cana,[173] Jesus' turning water to wine is sometimes approached allegorically. Jesus, a guest at the feast, changes 180 gallons of water into the best wine as a gift, when the regular wine had run out before the party was over (John 2:1–10).

An allegorical approach might argue:

> The wine that ran out represents the Jewish religion;
>
> The wedding guests picture religious people;
>
> That the wine ran out is saying that Judaism will not ultimately satisfy;
>
> The wine Jesus made is the new religion of Christianity;
>
> And more . . .

Perhaps one of the biggest reasons for not adopting such an approach to this story is that it is impossible for those who were there, at that moment, to have come away with these conclusions. We would have to assume that Jesus was orchestrating a dramatic "show" that would not have been understandable to those at the wedding feast, but that would only be able to be understood when some allegorical insights opened the narrative to those who were later to hear it or read it.

Because there is typically almost nothing in the narrative that provides the definitive key to the allegory, individual narratives can often end up being interpreted in a great variety of allegorical ways. The meaning of the narrative is only limited by the imaginative allegorizing of the reader.

WHAT YOU ALREADY KNOW ABOUT READING NARRATIVES

The truth is that you already know how to make sense of a narrative. You just need to do what you normally do with a narrative when you come to Gospel stories (or any Biblical narrative, for that matter). You make sense of narratives by learning from and learning through the experiences of others.

Perhaps you are planning on taking a trip to a well-known and popular amusement park with your family. In talking about it, some friends share their experience with their family at that particular amusement park. You listen to their story—*their narrative*. You pay attention to what they share about their experience. You seek to understand what they saw and heard and went through in their time at the park. You learn something about what the park is like, what the rides are like, what the crowds are like, and how your friends pursued their own adventure. You then make some plans for your own trip based on what you learned from their experiences.

But this doesn't mean 1) that the story of their experience will be identical to your own; 2) that you will need to ride the rides they did and follow the same plan they did; or 3) that you will have to go when they went, stay where they stayed, eat what they ate, etc. (As if their narrative were merely a collection of "life principles.") Nor do you hear their recounting of their adventure at the amusement park as if it were a veiled way for them to speak to you about how you are doing life and how you need to make different life choices. (As if their narrative were an allegory about your life.) Nevertheless, you can learn and personally take something away from the story they tell. Once you understand their narrative, you can make some application to your own situation.

The Gospels are not myths—fictional tales that are intended to illustrate and communicate truth about life.[174] The Gospels are not fables—moral tales told to help us learn to live good lives. The Gospels are not parables (although they do contain Jesus' parables)—pithy fictional stories that capture our attention with regard to spiritual realities.

The Gospels present us the truth about Jesus. They are made up of snapshots of the One who came to earth, ministered and taught and died and rose from the dead, and who lives forevermore. The Jesus we meet in the Gospel accounts is the risen Jesus who is still alive and who is still present and active in our world—although not in the incarnate way He was as seen in the Gospels. Through those snapshots—the verbal pictures telling us of His life, His teaching, His miracles, His ministry—we can come to know Jesus, and come to know Him better.

So, when approaching a Gospel narrative, read it as if it is a report of the real experiences of real people interacting with Jesus. Watch what happens. Listen to the exchange. Learn something from how Jesus interacts with them and how they interact with Him. And, above all else, come away impressed with Jesus. He is amazing!

APPENDIX THREE

USING THIS BOOK IN A SMALL GROUP SETTING

They were continually devoting themselves to the apostles' teaching and to fellowship, to the breaking of bread and to prayer.

—Acts 2:42

MANY CHRISTIAN COMMUNITIES HAVE COME to realize the benefit of small groups. Settings where Christians can gather to discuss and reflect on the Scriptures together, where individuals are free to ask questions and share thoughts, and where believers can pray into their own lives the truths they learn are a helpful piece of the discipleship puzzle.

With years of experience with small groups, I am convinced that every gathering of saints will benefit greatly from living together "in the Word." Like the early church that was devoted to "the apostles' teaching," healthy small group life grows out of a life shaped by the message of Jesus and the truth of Scripture. Such thinking has shaped the writing of this book.

Two of the primary goals in preparing this material are:

To help others think well about what Jesus reveals about Himself through the miracles He did; and

To encourage others to pay attention to what they read in the pages of Scripture and for them to become better readers of the Gospels.

With those goals in mind, it may be that this little book could be of benefit to a small group in their study and discussion of Scripture. But, in order to keep the main thing the main thing, the following suggestions are offered for using this book in small groups:

Do not lose sight of the primacy of the Scriptures. Each chapter in this book does contain portions of the Bible under discussion. What matters most are the words the Spirit inspired—the words of Scripture. The words of this author are neither inspired nor life-changing—God's Word is. So, however this book is used, it should be as an auxiliary to the Scripture, not in place of the Scriptures.

Do not overlook the value of reading Scripture together. Reading, listening to, hearing, and talking about the Scriptures is of vital importance. Even if the participants in the group have read this text, when it comes time to meet, reading the passages from the Bible and discussing what is there, in the pages of the Bible, should take priority. What insights might be found in this book should only be championed to the degree that they arise clearly from the Scriptures.

The group discussion questions at the end of each chapter are neither mandatory nor inspired. They are suggestions. They are intended to prompt interaction about what the Gospels tell us about a particular miracle and what that particular miracle reveals to us about Jesus. If the questions are helpful, feel free to use them. If they are not, you are obviously free to come up with your own.

Do not hesitate to debate, discuss, or disagree with what you read in this book. What matters most is that we grow to understand the Scriptures well and grow to know Jesus better. Allow the chapters in this book to nudge you towards those ends—even if you don't see eye to eye with this author. If, in the end, we disagree but you have wrestled well with what the Gospels say, you have thought deeply about what Jesus reveals to us in His miracles, and you have come to be more impressed and more in delighted in Him, then this book will have served its purpose well.

ENDNOTES

There is a three-fold purpose to these endnotes:

In working through the miracles of Jesus, there are times when issues arise which, although important, are tangential to the primary focus or central idea of the miracle account. These endnotes provide some reflection on many of those incidental topics and issues, and in so doing keep us from ignoring such issues entirely while not unduly cluttering the exposition and explanation of the miracle accounts.

When necessary or helpful, the endnotes provide technical clarification of terms or ideas presented in the body of the book, or point to additional resources that might be of benefit for further study.

As needed, the endnotes provide cross references—Biblical references which provide helpful clarification to something mentioned in the body of the book and internal cross references which call attention to places within the book where the topics in view in the endnote are addressed.

1. In writing about Jesus' stilling of the storm, Simon J. Kistemaker explains, "The disciples now saw a display of Jesus' divinity in action." (Simon J. Kistemaker, *The Miracles: Exploring the Mystery of Jesus' Divine Works* [Grand Rapids, MI: Baker, 2006], 22). Later, he notes that "Jesus walked on the water in the Lake of Galilee and identified himself as divine" (ibid., 32). With no intention of diminishing my regard for Dr. Kistemaker's contribution to the study of Jesus' miracles, conclusions such as these—that Jesus was in some way proving He was God by doing miracles—seem to cloud other things Jesus may actually be revealing in doing what He did.

2. See Appendix One for further thoughts on miracles in the lives of others.

3. It is beyond the scope of our present study to pursue the subject of miracles done through the agency of other supernatural powers, other than God Himself. But something should be said about the possibility that people other than those walking with God are able to do miraculous kinds of things. We see this, for example, in Mark 13:22 or Acts 19:13–14. But such superhuman deeds do testify that there is something beyond them—a supernatural power—at work. When supernatural power is at work, and when the character of the person betrays evidence of God's character, and when the miracle worker gives glory to God, the miracle attests that God is present and active.

4. Some of the works in print worth considering would include *Miracles* by C. S. Lewis (New York: HarperOne, 2001); *All the Miracles of the Bible* by Herbert Lockyer (Grand Rapids, MI: Zondervan, 1988); and *In Defense of Miracles* edited by R. Douglas Gievett and Gary Harbermas (Downers Grove, IL: InterVarsity Press, 1997).

5. It is interesting to note what Peter stated about Jesus and His miracles in Acts 2:22. His point would appear to be that the miracles Jesus did "attested to" God's support and involvement in Jesus' life. Peter doesn't directly derive from the miracles themselves that Jesus was, in fact, God come in the flesh. The issue at hand is to consider how we are to understand the miracles of Jesus. And Peter appears to come short of affirming that the miracles that Jesus did were obvious proof that He was God.

6. See, for example, John 10:25–38.

7. Although I begin this chapter with a question assuming that the reader will have some familiarity with the ministry of Jesus, I am not expecting every reader to be well acquainted with all of Jesus' miracles. Each miracle will be approached in a fresh way, including a recounting of the miracle account itself from the Gospels.

8. In reading the Gospels, we are not immediately aware that they are all not seamlessly woven into one chronological whole. As a result, there is some confusion about Jesus' first miracle. Some think it must have been when Jesus helped Peter by providing a miraculous catch of fish (Luke 5:1–11; a miracle we will look at later in this book). But John's language is clear. The miracle at the wedding feast in Cana is the first one Jesus did. He has not yet gathered the Twelve; the reference to the "disciples" who were with Him is not a reference to the Twelve but to the few who had begun to hang out with Him at this point. In this miracle, we do actually see the "first impression" made by Jesus.

9. An allegory is "a story where each element in the story means something quite foreign to the story itself" (Gordon Fee and Douglas Stuart, *How to Read the Bible for All Its Worth* (Grand Rapids, MI: Zondervan, 1982), 127). An allegory is a story that tells about something else, the elements of the story standing in for various components of the truth trying to be told. Such a treatment of this miracle tends to overlook the fact that this event actually happened; John is not merely "telling us a tale" to make a point. Jesus did what He did. And He did it for a reason that meant something to those who were there, in the situation. Jesus was not "using" the situation to say something entirely different.

10. I will be taking an approach to the Gospel accounts rooted in the conviction that they are accurate records of what actually happened. Some scholars view the Gospels as somewhat "free" collections prepared by sincere Christians who, nevertheless, had certain theological agendas that gave rise to not only the creative use of sources but also resulted in the wholesale creation of stories about Jesus that might not really be rooted in what happened in His life and ministry. It is beyond the scope of this work

to defend my approach to the Gospels, but it is important to note that I hold the accounts of the miracles we will be examining to be reliable records of what Jesus did and said and, thus, valuable windows into what Jesus wants to say to us. This approach also means that we need to give appropriate attention to how those present to what Jesus was saying and doing would have understood what was happening. We can only answer questions about what a particular passage means to us after we have wrestled with what that particular event would have meant to those present at the time. Although the Bible does speak to us in our lives and our situations, it does so consistent with what it spoke in the original events and setting.

11. The word translated "glory" speaks of the splendor or magnificence of something. We tend to equate the idea of glory with the idea that God has glory and conclude that glory speaks of God's "godness." Although God is glorious (that is, filled with magnificent splendor), the word itself doesn't always mean something like "that which shows forth from God." For example, we are told in 1 Corinthians 15:40–44 that various bodies have differing "glories." God is exceedingly glorious; His magnificence is unmatched.

12. For John to tell us that Jesus did this sign to "manifest" His glory, he is saying that Jesus did this to make known or put on display His glory. To make something manifest is to show it off, to make it clear. He is telling us that Jesus is making evident and visible something about Himself that makes Him glorious.

13. That is not to say that John never speaks of faith in a decisive, entering-into-life kind of way. Clearly this would seem to be the case in John 1:12, where John has in view the change in life that comes to those who "believe" (the same root word as "faith") in Jesus so as to become the children of God. This is also the idea in the passage taken from Jesus' exchange with Nicodemus: those who believe in Him will not perish but have everlasting life (John 3:16). One other passage might help illustrate this point. In John 20:30-31, John writes: "Therefore many other signs Jesus also performed in the presence of the disciples, which are not written in this book; but these have been written so that you may believe that Jesus is the Christ, the Son of God; and that believing you may have life in His name." This suggests that John's record of the words and works of Jesus is intended to have a

cumulative effect; each miracle, standing alone, does not convey all that we are to know about Jesus. The "signs" that Jesus did were intended to stir in His followers and watchers a confidence that they could trust Him with their lives. Taken together—all of Jesus' words and works recorded by John—the evangelist intends that what he has written will be used by the Spirit to bring people to a final and cumulative saving faith.

14. There are times when John is clearly speaking of "believing in" or "having faith in" Jesus where what is in view is a growing, deepening, increasing personal trust in Jesus. John does not seem to think of faith simply as a one-time act of volition wherein someone acknowledges certain truths about Jesus. For John, faith is seen as a vital and growing, deep and abiding confidence in, fidelity to, and reliance on Jesus Himself. This must be the sense of believing in John 2:23–24 where some "believed," but Jesus wouldn't trust Himself to them because He was aware that there was still something lacking in even those that so believed. We will see this illustrated even more clearly when we look at the miracle of the raising of Lazarus.

15. Jack Hayford, *Moments with Majesty* (Sisters, OR: Multnomah, 1990), 27.

16. In reading this miracle in this way, I am not suggesting this means we can have whatever we want from Jesus, as if He were some kind of celestial genie just waiting to grant us three wishes. What Jesus did He did in grace; He did what He did because He wanted to do it, not because someone "wished" or even asked for it. Although this miracle does demonstrate Jesus' gracious benevolence, we cannot conclude from what He did here that we can have our every whim.

17. Most English Bibles here have "LORD" (the word *Lord* but all in capital letters). This is a convention widely used in translation. This all-capitalized word stands in for the personal name of God, typically understood to be spelled YHWH and often written out as Yahweh. When Pharaoh announced that he did not know "the LORD," it would seem that he was saying that this particular God, the one Moses identified by name (see Exodus 3:15 where God makes His name known to Moses; "the LORD" also stands in for Yahweh), was one he did not know.

18. C. F. Keil and F. Delitzsch, *Commentary on the Old Testament* (Grand Rapids, MI: Eerdmans, 1976), 1:478.

19. The word Peter used here to address Jesus is somewhat unique. The word is found only in Luke and is only used by those speaking to Jesus (5:5; 8:24, 45; 9:33, 49; 17:13). It is not the typical word translated "Lord" that is often used by those addressing Jesus. This word was typically used to refer to an overseer, or someone who "stood over" another.

20. The language Luke uses suggests that Peter's boat was far enough out in the lake that they probably couldn't have been heard if they shouted. Thus, they signaled for the help they needed.

21. This explains, in part, why Jesus would not give the religious leaders of His day a "sign" when they asked for it. See, for example, Matthew 12:38–39. They wanted a random act of divine power to prove His claims. But Jesus didn't do the things He did for that reason. Jesus did what He did because it was a genuine expression of His character and in order to meet genuine needs He saw. He wouldn't jump through hoops and use divine power the way they wanted Him to. He wasn't given to "proving Himself" in that way.

22. Did you notice that both Jesus' first miracle with Peter and His last are built around Jesus doing better at Peter's business than Peter had? It is a fascinating way to bookend Peter's walk with Jesus. Peter enters into his life with Jesus through the miraculous catch of fish, the account we are reading. After the resurrection, toward the end of their time together, Peter has gone back to fishing and has spent the night in fruitless labor. Jesus, meanwhile, has found enough fish for breakfast for the hungry fisherman. Peter's best efforts, toiling through the night, bring no results . . . in both situations. But in both situations Jesus readily supplies what is needed, graciously ministering to Peter in Peter's own area of expertise.

23. In Mark 1:16–20, we find Jesus inviting four men—Simon (Peter), Andrew, James, and John—to join Him. This encounter was not a full and formal call to discipleship, seeing as that comes later in the Gospel (Mark 3:13–19).

24. That Jesus taught in the synagogue on this particular Sabbath might not have been, in itself, remarkable. On any given Sabbath, the ruler of the synagogue would ask any of the Jewish men in the congregation in attendance to read from the Scriptures and offer a lesson of sorts.

25. As recorded in Mark 1:21–28, as Jesus was teaching, a man "with an unclean spirit" was found to be in the synagogue and, with a word, Jesus delivered the man from his spiritual oppression.

26. Mark 1:30–31: "Now Simon's mother-in-law was lying sick with a fever; and immediately they spoke to Jesus about her. And He came to her and raised her up, taking her by the hand, and the fever left her, and she waited on them." We'll come back to this simple healing later in this chapter.

27. Carrying a sick person would have been considered work by the religious leaders, something that was not permitted on the Sabbath. Thus, the sick were not brought to Jesus until after the sun had set (because that marked the end of the Sabbath).

28. This decision means that Jesus apparently left some people in Capernaum with their needs unaddressed. It is worth noting that Jesus does, later, return to the city. However, He is not going to set up a healing center in Capernaum; His ministry is broader than that.

29. There appears to be a difference between what is identified as leprosy in Biblical times and how doctors currently understand leprosy. In the contemporary world, leprosy is still a serious illness, it is infectious, and lepers are often still ostracized.

30. See Leviticus 13 and 14 for the basic Old Testament instructions for dealing with leprosy.

31. Mark 1:40; 5:10, 12, 17, 18, 23; 6:56; 7:32; 8:22.

32. Mark 10:17 records a rich man coming to Jesus and falling on his knees before Him.

33. Church history suggests that Mark's Gospel draws on the preaching of Peter. Given this possibility, the eyewitness feel of this account could well be due to the impact this moment had on Peter as he stood watching Jesus interacting with a leper.

34. The same word is found in Mark 3:5 where Jesus commands a man with a withered hand to "stretch out your hand."

35. It is clear, from other passages in Mark, that Jesus does not have to touch someone to bring healing (e.g., Mark 2:10–12, where Jesus restores a lame man with a word or Mark 7:29, where a little girl is delivered from an evil spirit at a distance merely by Jesus' word).

36. Although the word Jesus uses can convey the idea of "bearing witness" (as in "witnessing about Jesus" or "telling others about Jesus"), the word simply means to "make a statement about." When Jesus tells the former leper to go and show himself to the priests and offer a sacrifice for his cleansing, the "testimony" mentioned is most likely his public statement of his cleansing before the proper authorities who could validate this testimony.

37. See the instructions in Leviticus 14.

38. The synagogue official would be a leader in a local synagogue, although not a priest, or rabbi, or scribe. His duties were primarily to keep the synagogue—the Jewish place of community life and learning—running smoothly. It was an important role, but not primarily a teaching role.

39. The synagogue official used an endearing term in speaking of his need; literally, he asks for help for "my *little* daughter." Luke highlights for us the fact that this little girl was the man's only daughter (Luke 8:42). That adds a little to our understanding of the passion and persistence of this man.

40. The word *touched* here is probably to be understood as much more than just a casual brush of the hand. The word carried the sense of "grasped." It was a decisive and deliberate act; it was an act of desperation and hope.

How long did her hand linger? We do not know. Did she hold on until she felt something in her body that convinced her that she was now well? The text does not tell us. We are not privy to the details of this private moment. But, she apparently grabbed Jesus' clothes as He passed by. She was intentional, purposeful.

41. There is something wonderful in Jesus speaking to this woman as "Daughter." Because of her condition, she has been an outcast and familyless for many years. To hear Him address her this way must have been wonderful and inviting.

42. According to verse 30, Jesus had conscious internal awareness that something had happened—He knew "power had gone out" from Him.

43. All disease did not affect social life in quite the same way. This woman's trouble was profound. To have a "flow of blood" would have rendered her spiritually unclean. To be unclean meant that you could not participate in the regular religious life or social life of Israel. This unclean status was not necessarily a punishment for some perceived sin (although some afflictions might have been understood that way). The unclean status preserved the hygiene and the ritual purity of the people. As someone deemed unclean, she had to keep herself separate from others and normal life for awhile and go through a series of sacrifices to again become ceremonially clean. Even if the blood wasn't flowing on a specific day, a period of time was necessary for her to go through purification before she could be embraced and welcomed into the life of the community of faith. Seeing as she had a regular problem with this blood flowing, she would have been constantly on the outside of community life looking in. She would never have been able to get fully through the ritual cleansing before the problem resurfaced, leaving her ever unclean. The details of the instructions in the Law for dealing with such a problem are found in Leviticus 15:19–27.

44. Although the specifics of the Law regarding people who were unclean did not proscribe divorcing a spouse who was regularly unclean, the rabbis taught that as a result of such an affliction as this woman had, her husband was free to divorce her. She, most likely, would have been shut out from all regular family life.

45. John 5:19.

46. Remember, as we noted in our reading of the miracle at the wedding feast of Cana, that to "believe" in Jesus is often understood in the Gospels as an expression of personal confidence and trust in Him. Although many come to believe in the sense of realizing and affirming that Jesus is God-come-in-the-flesh to be the Redeemer of mankind, each time faith in Jesus is spoken of we are not brought face to face with that kind of ultimate affirmation of faith. Many times in the Gospels the idea seems to be not so much an issue of affirming certain truths about Jesus, but considering Jesus as trustworthy as to His character and person and, then, trusting Him! I think that in this case, Jesus is not so much inviting Jairus to come to a particular theological conclusion about Himself but to really trust Him. Such trust might well be rooted in what Jairus does think, theologically, about Jesus, but the call is not to a doctrinal affirmation but to dependence and reliance on Jesus.

47. Mark wrote his Gospel in Greek and, thus, has translated all of Jesus' words into Greek. Although Jesus could well have spoken Greek, it is generally thought that among the Jewish people in Palestine, He most likely spoke Aramaic. In this passage, Mark has recorded for us the exact Aramaic words spoken by Jesus. If, as it is commonly held, that Mark wrote his Gospel based on the reminiscences of Peter, it may be that these very words so impressed Peter (one of the eyewitnesses) that Mark included them in his Gospel just as Peter would have told the account. The word "Talitha" is a diminutive; it means something like "little lamb" or "little dear one." Don't miss this marvelous picture. Jesus taking this small girl by the hand, holding her hand in His, and leaning over, He calls to her: "Little lamb, arise!"

48. Some commentators have noted the similarities between these two interwoven miracles. For example, the woman had suffered for 12 years and the little girl was 12. Both cases were considered hopeless. The woman grabbed hold of Jesus, while Jesus took the little girl's hand. In both instances, Jesus addressed the one for whom He had done something marvelous with an endearing term. Although these points are true, they are not principally what holds the two accounts together.

49. Although, at times, the headings found in many Bibles alerting the reader to what he or she is about to read can be helpful, the headings themselves are not inspired. Often—although not always—such headings provide only a superficial or simplistic assessment of what the particular passages is about.

50. Some of this material is a recap of what we explored in chapter 3, "It Would Have Been Risky."

51. There are a number of passages in the Scriptures that suggest there are times when sickness is, in some way, tied to sin. We see this in John 5:14 and, perhaps, James 5:13–15. However, all infirmity is not the result of sin. We can see this idea in passages like Job 2:1–8; John 9:1–7; and 1 Timothy 5:23.

52. As we saw in Chapter 3, "It Would Have Been Risky."

53. This is not to deny that Jesus at times does have divine insight. Examples are in Luke 6:8; John 1:48; 2:23–25; 13:19. Even in such cases, Jesus may not be pulling out His "God card." The Spirit could have mediated the supernatural knowledge He displays, an idea hinted at in passages such as Luke 4:18; 10:21.

54. This story provides us with the first mention of personal faith in Mark. It is unlikely that this reference to the faith of the four means they fully understood who Jesus was; faith wasn't an issue of merely getting Jesus' identity correct. In a later passage in Mark (4:35–41), Jesus questions the faith of His disciples. The lack of faith in that passage can serve as a parallel to this passage; in both passages the evidence of faith is seen in actions.

55. Mark mentions "faith" or "believing" (translations of the same Greek root word) in 1:15; 2:5; 4:40; 5:34, 36; 9:23, 42; 10:52; 11:22–24, 31; 13:21; 15:31; 16:13; and 16:14, 16. This passage is the first one in Mark that pictures someone "believing" or "having faith."

56. Blasphemy is mentioned only a few times in the Gospels: Matthew 12:31; 26:65; Mark 2:7; 14:64; Luke 22:65; John 10:33, 36.

57. See, for example, the instructions about sacrifices for forgiveness as found in Leviticus 1–4.

58. Anchored in Old Testament prophecies, the Jews were anticipating the coming of a divinely appointed deliverer. This God-given leader was referred to as the *Messiah* (the English pronunciation of a Hebrew word that means “anointed one”); in the New Testament this title is often rendered *Christ* (the English pronunciation of the a Greek word equivalent to the Hebrew term).

In the Old Testament, Israel’s priests (e.g., Exodus 28:41; 29:7; 30:30-33; Leviticus 4:3; 6:22; 8:12) and Israel’s prophets (e.g., 1 Kings 19:16; Isaiah 61:1; Psalm 105:15) and Israel’s kings (e.g., Judges 9:8; 1 Samuel 10:1; 16:13; 24:10; 26:11 1 Kings 1:34; 2 Kings 9:6–13) were often marked out for their particular God-given place of service through some kind of anointing. The Messiah came to be understood as the future, promised servant of God who would minister to the people of God in ways similar to all three of these offices and, in so doing, usher in the final phase of God’s universal plan.

59. Earlier in Mark, we find a few references to “authority” where evidence of divinity may not be in view (1:22, 27). Later in Mark, Jesus will grant authority to His disciples to carry out ministry (6:7); they will have a delegated right to act. That idea of delegated right to act may be the best way to understand Jesus’ claim to have authority to forgive sins in this passage.

60. Mark mentions others who were amazed by Jesus; see Mark 2:12; 3:21; 5:42; 6:51.

61. It was not uncommon in Jesus’ day (and not altogether absent in ours) for people to think that if there was something physically wrong with you, you must be under God’s judgment for something you did. This is clearly reflected in the disciples’ question in John 9:2 regarding whose sin was responsible for a man to have been born blind. Thus, this deformity left the man not only in a place of disdainful looks for his affliction, but perhaps also opened him to rumors and innuendos about what sin would result in such an affliction.

62. Although it is true, as has been noted, that Jesus often healed large numbers of people at one time (e.g., Matthew 12:15), there are instances recorded in the Gospels where He apparently did not heal all who were in need of healing, even given the opportunity. (See, for example, Mark 1:34-38; 3:9–10; 6:5. Mark's language suggests that not all who might have been in need of healing were, in fact, healed.)

63. It is interesting to note that the religious leaders were there, in the synagogue, with the expectation that Jesus might, in fact, heal someone. There are some Christians who have seemingly missed the significant role that physical healing had in the ministry of Jesus. It was so much a part of Jesus' public ministry that the religious leaders anticipated that He would heal, given the chance. This idea—that Jesus' reputation for healing was widespread and warranted—is reflected in a number of places in the New Testament. For example, Peter can speak of Jesus' ministry of "doing good" and healing (Acts 10:38) as something that was well known to Cornelius and his household in Caesarea.

64. The religious leaders' trap laid for Jesus had to do with "Sabbath keeping." The Old Testament law proscribed that no work should be done on the Sabbath (Exodus 20:9–11). As the rabbis explained what this meant, they overlaid this simple instruction with a range of descriptions to delineate what constituted work. They did recognize that if someone's life were in jeopardy, even on the Sabbath work could be done to save him. However, they did not see mere healing as necessary for saving a life, so they would consider the effort undertaken to heal someone to be work, and thus unlawful on the Sabbath.

65. For example, see Mark 1:44, 7:36, and Luke 8:56. There is some debate within the community of believing Bible teachers as to why Jesus wanted to keep some miracles secret. No attempt will be made to resolve this issue here, only to note that there were times when Jesus apparently was not interested in calling attention to what He had done.

66. This is the idea found in Paul's words in Ephesians 2:4–7, where he announces that what God is doing in redeeming people is putting the surpassing riches of His grace on display.

67. For example, see Mark 4:10, 34.

68. Although Jesus does select twelve men to become an identifiable band of disciples, He selected them out of the large number of followers (Mark 3:7–19; Luke 6:12–16), He does at times include others in His discussion with the Twelve (Mark 4:10: Luke 10:1–5), He calls others along with the Twelve to a life of following (Mark 8:34–38), and He commissions them to teach others all that He taught them (Matthew 28:18–20). It is clear that although there is something special about the relationship the Twelve had with Jesus, they are prototypical of all disciples.

69. In order to best understand a Gospel passage, it is helpful to use one's "sanctified imagination" and picture what it would have been like to be in the particular scene being described. The goal is not to pretend, but to grasp the reality of what was being experienced by those in the account. Seeing as the Gospels record what really happened to real people, picturing ourselves there can aid us in grasping the situation in all its realness.

70. Mark 1:16–20.

71. Luke 5:5.

72. Given the particular geographical setting for the Sea of Galilee, it is prone to sudden and severe storms. Since a number of the disciples were long-time fishermen of that lake, they would have been experienced in dealing with its stormy conditions.

73. James 2:19.

74. In Mark 4, we read about Jesus' teaching about "the sower [who] sows the word." As Jesus explains this parable, He underscores the importance of hearing—giving attention to the word that is sown. He follows this up with some other short parables about how the word sown bears fruit, even if it is unclear how it will grow (4:26-34). Throughout the passage, we find Jesus repeatedly emphasizing the importance of giving heed to His words (4:3, 9, 20, 24, 33). Among other points that Jesus is making, the idea of being attentive to Jesus' words is central to the teaching.

75. Psalm 46:10; Mark 10:45; Matthew 28:20.

76. Matthew 28:20.

77. Hebrews 7:25.

78. *The Sound of Music*, directed by Robert Wise (1965).

79. There are a number of places where Jesus heals someone with only a word; for example, see Matthew 8:5–13 and 15:21–28.

80. R. C. Trench, *Notes on the Miracles of our Lord* (Grand Rapids, MI: Baker, 1949), 219–220.

81. The word often carries a sense of "throwing" or "tossing" and not simply "touching." For example, the word is used by Mark to speak of fishermen casting a net into the sea (1:16), a sower who throws seed out (4:26), and a demon who tossed a young child into the fire (9:22).

82. Some translations render this phrase to suggest that Jesus touched the man's tongue with the saliva. The language does not require this. I believe that the best way to understand what Mark wrote is that Jesus spit and then simply touched the man's tongue with His finger.

83. Although we commonly refer to this man as one who is "dumb" (i.e., mute, unable to speak), the text suggests that he might not have been totally unable to make sounds. Nevertheless, it is clear that he was unable to verbally communicate in anything resembling an articulate or intelligible way. Notice that in his healing the result was that he was able to "speak plainly." Herbert Lockyer notes: "Evidently the man was unable to utter articulate and intelligible sounds" (*All the Miracles of the Bible* [Grand Rapids, MI: Zondervan, 1961], 207).

84. It is important to note something about the character of this miracle. Notice how this man is not only healed of his affliction but also made completely whole. This is quite amazing. He is not only no longer deaf and dumb, but he can now speak plainly. Jesus does not merely give the man

the use of his ears and his vocal chords; Jesus miraculously infuses into the man whatever was necessary for him to speak as plainly and clearly as someone who had never been deaf and dumb.

85. There are a number of passages where Jesus indicates that the faith of the one He is ministering to has a part to play in what happens. For example, see Mark 9:20–22 and the woman healed of a flow of blood, Matthew 15:21–28 and the deliverance brought to the daughter of a Gentile woman, and Mark 10:46–52, where Jesus heals Bartimaeus of blindness.

86. There are other passages in the Gospels where it appears that Jesus is creating an opportunity for someone to exercise faith. Perhaps one of the more notable is the exchange Jesus has with the Syrophoenician woman in Mark 7, a miracle we will examine later. See Chapter 10, "What About the Crumbs?"

87. This idea of Jesus ministering to the whole person and not just the afflicted body of the person is clearly seen when, confronted with the paralytic lowered through the roof by his friends, Jesus simply says to him that his sins are forgiven (Mark 2:1–5). That is not to say that Jesus was not, all along, intending to fully heal the man, but only to note that Jesus addressed something other than the obvious physical need.

88. Perhaps one of the more notable examples is Luke 7:11–15, where Jesus raises a widow's son from the dead. There is no indication in the passage that anyone either anticipated Jesus to do anything or believed in Him for this astounding work of grace. From what Luke tells us, this miracle was prompted by Jesus' compassion.

89. See John 8:28–29 and 14:10.

90. *The Elephant Man*, directed by David Lynch (Paramount, 1980).

91. Peter's confession that Jesus is the "Son of God" is connected with Peter's recognition that Jesus is the Messiah (or Christ). We must be willing to grant that Peter understands something about what he is saying, but it is not likely that he has a full grasp of all that is entailed in confessing that Jesus is the Son of God. Peter sees some things about Jesus and has

received sufficient grace from God to make this acknowledgement, even if he doesn't grasp the totality of the confession.

92. After affirming Peter's confession, Jesus explains that His Messianic call includes suffering and death. This is not acceptable to Peter. We are not told why Peter balks at this, but it is likely that his understanding of the Messiah, drawing on his understanding of the Old Testament, drove Peter to the idea that Messiah would come as a victorious king/warrior. Thus, if Jesus was the Messiah, the idea that He would be put to death would have been unimaginable to Peter.

93. We read that Jesus came walking on the water at the "fourth watch of the night" (14:25). That would be between 3:00 and 6:00 in the morning.

94. When the disciples saw the figure walking on the water, Matthew tells us they were "terrified" (14:26)—a word that describes a state of great agitation. It's the word used to speak of the troubled state of Herod's soul when he heard that a king had been born—a king who could ultimately upset his own rule (Matthew 2:3). In approaching the disciples in the boat, Jesus has to tell them to "take courage" and to stop being afraid (14:27). All of this language tells us that the disciples were in a tremendous state of agitation and fear when Jesus comes to them.

95. The account of the stilling of the storm is found in Matthew 8:23–27 and Mark 4:36–41. It is addressed in chapter 7, "What Would You Have Done?"

96. We are given only a little insight into Peter's experience. After climbing out of the boat, we read that Peter "walked on the water and came toward Jesus." This suggests that he had more than a momentary standing on the surface of the water. He was making progress toward Jesus. But, after at least a few moments, he was "beginning to sink." I am not sure how we should picture that. How far did Peter slip into the water before he cried out? Did the water reach his knees? His hips? When did he realize that he was, perhaps, in danger? We are not told specifically. But he did have the adventure of walking toward Jesus, on his own, before he began to fear and then to sink.

97. Jesus speaks to Peter as one who is "little-faithed" (14:31). This is a compound word that does not imply that Peter was completely devoid of faith. This sense of "littleness" is seen in the way the prefix used in this compound word is used to speak of "few" laborers (not no laborers; Matthew 9:37), and the "few" fish at the disposal of the disciples for the feeding of the multitude (not no fish at all; Matthew 15:34). This passage does not resolve the full reason for Peter's smallness of faith or struggle in continuing to walk on water. Peter noticed the waves roaring around him; he did begin to fear. Those things could have contributed to his faith struggle, but the passage does not make explicit what hindered his little-faithed-ness from blossoming into the fullness of faith that would have been needed to keep on walking on the water. It is evident from other passages of Scripture that difficulties and fear are not necessarily the things that overthrow faith. One place this is evident in Matthew is at the end of the Gospel, where we read that the centurion and other soldiers watching over Jesus' crucifixion and death "became very frightened" (the same word used of Peter's fear in walking on the water) but then proceeded to affirm of Jesus, "Truly this was the Son of God" (Matthew 27:54).

98. Matthew 16:15–23.

99. Matthew 17:19–20.

100. See Mark 5:35–43. This miracle is discussed in chapter 4, "Just a Moment, Please."

101. Matthew 17:1–8.

102. See, for example, Acts 4:36 where Barnabas is referred to as the "son of encouragement" and Matthew 13:38 where Jesus speaks of "sons of the evil one."

103. Luke 9:54.

104. Mark 10:35–37.

105. Jerome S. Bruner and Leo Postman, "On the Perception of Incongruity: A Paradigm," *Journal of Personality,* 18 (1949), 206–223.

106. Ibid., 222.

107. To identify the woman as a Canaanite indicates that she was a descendant of those whom the Israelites were to have driven out when they settled in the Promised Land after the Exodus (Deuteronomy 20:17; Joshua 3:10). The dispossession of the Canaanites was never complete; their influence continued to be felt (Joshua 16:10; 17:13). Historically, they were polytheistic and embraced both temple prostitution and child sacrifice in their worship practices. The references in the Old Testament to the worship of Ba'al can provide some insight into what would have been Canaanite religious practices.

108. The word is used this way in Matthew in 13:27; 18:25, 27; 20:28. It is also likely that others who addressed Jesus as "Lord" early in the Gospel accounts were using a title of respect and were not affirming His full divinity (e.g., Matthew 8:2, 6, 8, 21).

109. In Matthew 12:23, when a group of Jewish people who had been following Jesus and watching His ministry ask, "This man cannot be the Son of David, can He?", they are probably using that title in a Messianic way. Clearly, when Jesus comes into Jerusalem in what is often referred to as His "triumphal entry," the cry of the people "Hosanna to the Son of David" is a Messianic cry (Matthew 21:9).

110. When the angel, speaking to Joseph, refers to him as "Son of David," the title does not mean the angel thought Joseph was the Messiah (Matthew 1:20). Joseph was, however, a distant descendant of David.

111. When Jesus commissioned and sent out the Twelve, He specifically instructed them to go "to the lost sheep of the house of Israel" (Matthew 10:7). Even though Jesus' ministry was focused in Palestine, His reputation had spread as far as the Roman province of Syria (4:23–25), where the cities of Tyre and Sidon were located.

112. Jesus did heal and minister to Gentiles who were brought to Him or who came to Him (4:24–25; 8:5–10), but the focus of His public ministry was with the Jewish people.

113. The word translated "to bow down" in this passage pictures kneeling down or bowing down before someone. There are a number of places in Matthew where the sense of the word is more likely something akin to "worship" (Matthew 2:2, 8, 11; 4:9), although in this passage it cannot be insisted that the woman is actually worshipping Jesus. She is, at least, humbling herself before Him, as others have in Matthew's Gospel (Matthew 8:2; 9:18).

114. The only times anyone specifically is referred to as a "dog" in the Gospels are in this passage and the parallel passage in Mark 7:24–30. There are a few places in the New Testament where those who are opposed to the truth of the Gospel are referred to as "dogs" (see Philippians 3:2; Revelation 22:15).

115. A. T. Robertson, *Word Pictures in the New Testament,* (Grand Rapids, MI: Baker, 1930), I:125. The specific word that Jesus uses here (and the woman uses in her reply) is the diminutive form of the basic word for dog; that is, the word here might be translated "little dog" or "household dog." Some see significance in that Jesus did not use the more common word for dog—a word that would have been more fitting for the dogs in the street or for wild dogs.

116. Jesus identifies only two individuals in the Gospels as having "great" faith. This woman is one; the other is a centurion who approached Jesus on behalf of a sick servant (Matthew 8:5–13; Luke 7:1–10). The woman's faith is "great," says Jesus, using a word that refers to her faith as "substantial or large." Jesus says that the centurion's faith is "great," but there uses a word that pictures the greatness more in terms of quantity or degree. It is fascinating to note that of those who came to Jesus and were identified with an extraordinary degree of faith, the two individuals so identified were both Gentiles.

117. See Chapter 3: *It Would Have Been Risky.*

118. Michael P. Borgia, *Human Vision and the Night Sky: How to Improve Your Observing Skills* (New York: Springer Science, 2006), 3.

119. Mark 3:13–19.

120. Mark 6:7–13.

121. The word *apostle* means "one sent." It refers to someone who has a delegated assignment and authority. It's interesting to note that Mark only uses the word *apostle* to refer to the twelve close followers of Jesus twice: once when they are first identified (Mark 3:14 as found in some manuscripts of Mark); as found in some early manuscripts of the Gospel and once when they are returning from the teaching and healing "tour of duty" they were given (Mark 6:30).

122. A denarius was what a typical day-laborer made for one day's work. Two hundred denarii would be something close to a year's wages for the average worker. Seeing as Jesus had sent His disciples out on their mission trip with instructions to take nothing with them and to not take any money (see Mark 6:7–8), their reactionary response probably should be understood as a bit sarcastic. They don't have any money; clearly they aren't carrying a year's wages in the pockets of their robes.

123. When thinking of the five loaves and two fish, we shouldn't think about what you would find in your local grocery store. The loaves would not likely be what we conceive of as loaves of bread, but more like a pita, or small, round, flat bread. The fish were probably small salted fish, something one might carry in a pack on a short journey.

124. Formally, the tense used is called the *aorist* tense. Technically it pictures an event in its entirety. It is commonly translated as a simple past tense in English.

125. Mark 6:45–46. For the miracle that happens after this feeding, see Chapter 9, "In Over Your Head."

126. For example, see Mark 1:27; 2:12; 5:42.

127. The same word is used in 6:31, 32, and 35, referring to the place they were, although some English translations use differing words in those verses.

128. I have heard some teachers explain that the disciples, having recently returned from their healing and teaching opportunity, should have (could have?) understood that they had the power to meet this need in a miraculous way. Personally, I find that such insight on their behalf is highly unlikely. There is nothing in what they had experienced that would have set them up to think they could miraculously produce (or even multiply) food for the multitude.

129. Mark 14:41.

130. Mark 8:1–10. In Mark 8:15–21, as Jesus talks with His disciples He reminds them of a couple of miracles. Of all the amazing things He has done, He only asked them to recall two in particular—the two feedings. Nowhere else in the Gospels does Jesus invite His disciples to reflect on His miracles. But apparently the two feedings—the one here in Mark 6 and a subsequent one in Mark 8—have some significant benefit to the disciples. They should have been learning from these miracles. These miracles were not simply or solely about meeting the need of a crowd, but were intended to be for the disciples' direct benefit and instruction.

131. Mark 8:15–21.

132. I am not suggesting that a simple word count is the critical component in understanding a passage of Scripture or indicative of the relative importance of a particular section. If that were the case, the passion and death of Jesus would be significantly less important than Jesus' Sermon on the Mount. But such is, obviously, not the case. I am suggesting that if we read the account of the raising of Lazarus as if it is only about affirming Jesus' power over death (and, thus, proving His divine status), than it would seem that John spent a great deal of time and effort (evident in the number of words he used) on things that seem incidental to that point. That John gave so much attention to Jesus' interaction with Martha leads me to

think that their exchange is crucial to what John wants to communicate and, even more importantly, what Jesus is concerned with.

133. Mark 1:32–39.

134. Mark 5:21–43; see Chapter 4, "Just a Moment, Please" for a discussion of this miracle.

135. We can assume that Martha's remark about Lazarus being the one whom Jesus loved is true. Apparently Jesus had a close and affectionate friendship with Lazarus and his family.

136. Some might conclude from what Jesus says about Lazarus' sickness being "not unto death" that Jesus was wrong. Lazarus did die. However, Jesus might well have been meaning that Lazarus' sickness would not *end* in his death—and although he did die, that is not where this sickness ended. Lazarus walked out of the tomb—and walked away from the sickness—alive.

137. In Jesus' day there was debate among the Jewish leaders regarding the reality of the resurrection. Some affirmed that there would be a resurrection; others did not. This is seen in Acts 23:6–8 where the Sadducees and the Pharisees are on opposite sides of the debate. There are a few Old Testament references that would have given some grounds for Martha's affirmation of a future resurrection: Isaiah 26:19–21; Ezekiel 37:12–14; Daniel 12:1–3; and Job 19:25–27.

138. The question asked by the mourners at Lazarus' home suggests that Jesus' reputation as an effective healer was well-known and warranted.

139. Jesus' words found in John 5:19; 8:28; and 14:10 make it clear that Jesus does what He does because of what the Father wants of Him.

140. Although Martha can and does make such clear declarations of what she understands about Jesus, we have to remember that she does not likely understand the full implications of all she is affirming. She does not know all that we, as readers of the New Testament, know about Jesus.

141. As noted in the chapter "And So It Begins," the display of glory is not necessarily "proof of divinity." For Jesus to refer to seeing the glory of God, He is referring to a display of some quality of character of God.

142. For example, see Matthew 24:13–15, 23–25; Luke 12:1.

143. There are a number of passages where it does not appear that the Pharisees, in particular, are being singled out as hypocrites. For example, see Matthew 7:1–5; Luke 12:54–56.

144. Simon the Pharisee's invitation to Jesus to share a meal appears to be sincere (Luke 7:36–50).

145. John 3:1–21.

146. According to Acts 15:5, some of the Pharisees did, in fact, become followers of Jesus.

147. By resisting the stereotype that all Pharisees were steeped in hypocrisy, we are freed to understand the question they raised about Jesus' forgiving the paralyzed man of his sins as a legitimate concern, rather than an argumentative, baiting confrontation. See the discussion in Chapter 5, "More Than Anticipated."

148. Matthew 10:2–4; Mark 3:16–19; Luke 6:13–16.

149. One commentator's take on Thomas' words is to remark: "Thomas rather gloomily said to the rest, 'Let us go, too, so that we may die with Him.'" (Leon Morris, *Reflections on the Gospel of John* [Grand Rapids, MI: Baker, 1988], 4:714.

150. "Thomas apparently did not expect Jesus to survive another trip to hostile Jerusalem. Yet, to his credit, Thomas was resolved to go with Jesus though it might cost him his life." (J. Carl Laney, *Moody Gospel Commentary: John* [Chicago: Moody Press, 1992], 206.)

151. Jesus had appeared to His disciples, without Thomas in attendance, in John 20:19–23.

152. John's language in referring to the door being "shut" indicates that the door was securely closed; think "locked tight."

153. Matthew 26:31; Mark 14:27.

154. John 13:21–22, 38.

155. Luke 22:39–46.

156. "Thomas has often been criticized as a 'doubter' and a 'skeptic' for refusing to believe the bodily resurrection of Jesus without tangible proof. It should be remembered that none of the disciples had any concept of the resurrection prior to the event. Thomas was not [an] exception." (Laney, *John*, 368)

157. Chapter 12, "It's Who You Know."

158. In the New Testament, the words translated "believe", "belief", and "faith" all come from a common root word.

159. "Be diligent to present yourself approved to God as a workman who does not need to be ashamed, accurately handling the word of truth" (2 Timothy 2:15). "Like newborn babies, long for the pure milk of the word, so that by it you may grow in respect to salvation" (1 Peter 2:2).

160. "I will meditate on Your precepts and regard Your ways" (Psalm 119:15). "You search the Scriptures because you think that in them you have eternal life; it is these that testify about Me; and you are unwilling to come to Me so that you may have life" (John 5:39–40). For a book-length treatment on the need for Christians to think well, see John Piper, *Think: The Life of the Mind and the Love of God* (Wheaton, IL: Crossway, 2010).

161. "Open my eyes, that I may behold wonderful things from Your law" (Psalm 119:18). "But when He, the Spirit of truth, comes, He will guide you

into all the truth" (John 16:13). "Consider what I say, for the Lord will give you understanding in everything" (2 Timothy 2:7).

162. "Let the word of Christ richly dwell within you, with all wisdom teaching and admonishing one another" (Colossians 3:16).

163. With regard to the miracle at the wedding feast in Cana, one commentator wrote that Jesus, "as the Lord and the Creator of all nature . . . overleaps the elements of time, growth, gathering, crushing, and fermentation. He takes water . . . and without a word or gesture, in utter simplicity, the water becomes wine. Thus He demonstrated His authority—as God!—over the processes of nature." (Ray C. Stedman, *God's Loving Word: Exploring the Gospel of John* [Grand Rapids, MI: Discovery House, 1993], 71) A similar approach is taken in a commentary on Matthew where the author, in explaining Jesus' walking on the water, says that "to walk on the sea and to still a storm are prerogatives that belong only to God" and that this miracle is, fundamentally, a "divine act." (David L. Turner, *Cornerstone Biblical Commentary: The Gospel of Matthew* [Carol Stream, IL: Tyndale House, 2005], 205.) Jesus is, without doubt or debate, divine. The question in view is whether proving His divinity is the most fruitful way of understanding His miracles. David Otto, in *The Miracles of Jesus* (Abingdon, 2000), explores a number of the miracles of Jesus with an eye on what they tell us about Jesus, but he seems to focus on issues of Jesus' identity and interprets many of the miracles as almost symbolic acts, intended to change His viewers understanding of things like the Law and the Sabbath. Richard Phillips wrote *Mighty to Save: Discovering God's Grace in the Miracles of Jesus* (n.p.: P & R Publishing, 2001) focusing on the miracles found only in Luke. With that Lucan perspective, he looks at the miracles in terms of how they enlighten our understanding of Jesus' work to save sinners.

164. See the Introduction, "With a Focus On Him."

165. It is beyond the scope of this book to present a systematic defense of Jesus' full divinity. A few of the many passages that, taken together, rightly affirm the deity of Jesus are Isaiah 9:6–7; John 20:28; Colossians 1:15–20; 2:9; Titus 2:13; and 2 Peter 1:1.

166. Chapter 5, "More Than Anticipated."

167. When drawing on the full witness of the New Testament, the title "Son of Man" may convey something about Jesus' divine nature. This seems to be what Stephen has in mind when he spoke of "the Son of Man standing at the right hand of God" (Acts 7:56). In the opening chapters of the letter to the Hebrews, the author is arguing for Jesus' supremacy over all, leading to an understanding of His divine nature. In those early chapters, the author of the letter to the Hebrews does quote Psalm 8:4, referring to Jesus as the "Son of Man." Also, there are two references in the Revelation where Jesus is referred to as the "Son of Man" (Revelation 1:13; 14:14), references that appear to have Jesus' divine nature in view. However, when those who encounter Jesus in the Gospels use the title, it may carry more of a Messianic sense—not devoid of divine overtones but perhaps not clearly a divine title. In the Old Testament, God uses the title "son of man" to refer to the prophet Ezekiel over ninety times. Used of the prophet, the title means something like "one uniquely related to mankind" (as God's prophetic spokesman).

168. The only book-length treatment of the Spirit's work in and through the life of Jesus is Gerald Hawthorne's excellent book *The Presence and the Power: The Significance of the Holy Spirit in the Life and Ministry of Jesus* (Eugene, OR: Wipf and Stock, 2003).

169. Mark 6:7–13.

170. Luke 10:1–17.

171. Acts 6:8; 8:6.

172. Matthew 14:23–25; Luke 6:12.

173. Chapter One, "And So It Begins."

174. Liberal theologians defended the idea that the Gospels are "mythic." They argued for a distinction between the truth the Gospel stories communicated (called *Geschichte* and referring to the essential truth convey by the Gospel stories) and the historical recounting of the life

and ministry of Jesus (called *Historie* and referring to the truthfulness of the historical account). Rudolph Bultmann, in *Die Geschichte der synoptischen Tradition* (1921, 1931; an English translation of Bultman's work was published by Harper in 1976 entitled *The History of the Synoptic Tradition*) and an essay published in 1941 entitled *Neues Testament und Mythologie* (an English translation was published in a collection in 1961) sought to make the case that the Gospels were, fundamentally, mythical—offering the readers *Geschichte* truth while not being *Historie* truth. For such interpreters, the Gospel stories have value not in what they tell us about the historical person Jesus, but what the proclamation of the message associated with Jesus means for us today.

For more information about
Brian Onken
and
More Than His God Card
please visit:

www.theriverupstate.org
www.facebook.com/TheRiverUpstate

Brian can be reached at

brianonken55@gmail.com

For more information about
AMBASSADOR INTERNATIONAL
please visit:

www.ambassador-international.com
@AmbassadorIntl
www.facebook.com/AmbassadorIntl